Re-thinking History

Re-thinking History

Keith Jenkins

ROUTLEDGE

London and New York *1991*

First published 1991
by Routledge
11 New Fetter Lane, London EC4P 4EE

Simultaneously published in the USA and Canada
by Routledge
a division of Routledge, Chapman and Hall, Inc.
29 West 35th Street, New York, NY 10001

Photoset and printed in Great Britain by
Redwood Press Limited, Melksham, Wiltshire

British Library Cataloguing in Publication Data
Jenkins, Keith
  Re-thinking history.
  1. Historiography
  I. Title
  907

Library of Congress Cataloging in Publication Data
Jenkins, Keith
  Re-thinking history/Keith Jenkins.
    p. cm.
  Includes bibliographical references and index.
  1. History – Philosophy. 2. History – Methodology. 3. History –
  Study and teaching.   I. Title.
  D16.8.J386   1991
  901–dc20   91–10051

ISBN 0–415–06778–2

For Maureen, Philip and Patrick

Contents

Acknowledgements

Some of the arguments run in this book have appeared in slightly
different forms in other places, most notably in the journal *Teaching History*. But whether they have appeared in print or not they
have all been semi-publicly aired in the teaching of various
groups of students over the last few years, and I would like to
thank them for engaging in some wide-ranging debates. My
thanks too to friends who have discussed with me most of the
issues that are considered in this book: Keith Grieves, John
McKenzie, Guy Nelson and Richard Pulley. For some years I
have benefited from the collaboration of Peter Brickley, and what
appears here bears more than a passing resemblance both to his
ideas and to his constructive criticism.

Keith Jenkins
January 1991

Every discipline, I suppose, is, as Nietzsche saw most clearly, constituted by what it *forbids* its practitioners to do. Every discipline is made up of a set of restrictions on thought and imagination, and none is more hedged about with taboos than professional historiography – so much so that the so-called 'historical method' consists of little more than the injunction to 'get the story straight' (without any notion of what the relation of 'story' to 'fact' might be) and to avoid both conceptual overdetermination and imaginative excess (i.e., 'enthusiasm') at any price.

Yet the price paid is a considerable one. It has resulted in the repression of the *conceptual apparatus* (without which atomic facts cannot be aggregated into complex macrostructures and constituted as objects of discursive representation in a historical narrative) and the remission of the *poetic moment* in historical writing to the interior of the discourse (where it functions as an unacknowledged – and therefore uncriticizable – *content* of the historical narrative).

Those historians who draw a firm line between history and philosophy of history fail to recognise that every historical discourse contains within it a full-blown, if only implicit, philosophy of history.... The principal difference between history and philosophy of history is that the latter brings the conceptual apparatus by which the facts are ordered in the discourse to the surface of the text, while history proper (as it is called) buries it in the interior of the narrative, where it serves as a hidden or implicit shaping device....

Hayden White, Tropics of Discourse, pp. 126–7

Introduction

This book is addressed primarily to students who are embarking upon a study of the question, 'what is history?' It has been written both as an introduction (in the literal sense that there may be some points in what follows that have not been encountered before) and as a polemic. In the following pages I am running a particular argument as to what I think history is, not that you should accept it but rather that you might engage critically with it. The aim, throughout, is to help in the development of your own self-consciously held (reflexive) position on history . . . to be in control of your own discourse.[1]

Both these things – an introductory text and a polemic – seem to me to be necessary at this point in time. For although there are introductory texts on the market already, popular primers such as Edward Carr's *What Is History?*, Geoffrey Elton's *The Practice of History* and Arthur Marwick's *The Nature of History*[2] these, despite their sometime revision, still carry with them the ballast of their formative years (the 1950s and 1960s) such that they have now effectively become old favourites. They are also in a sense (as are more recent additions to the genre such as John Tosh's *The Pursuit of History*[3]) very 'English' texts, a characteristic which has had the somewhat unfortunate consequence of helping isolate history from some of the wider and arguably more generous intellectual developments that have recently been taking place in related discourses. Both philosophy and literature, for example, have engaged very seriously with the question of what is the nature of their own nature.[4]

It might therefore well be argued that history is, *vis-à-vis* these neighbouring discourses, theoretically backward, a remark that perhaps calls for an immediate illustration in order to prevent any misunderstandings.

If you go into an academic bookshop and look over the shelves occupied by texts on philosophy, you will find a vast array of works wherein the problem of the foundations and limits of what can be known and what can be done 'philosophically' are the staple diet: texts on ontology (theories of being), epistemology (theories of knowledge) and methodology; texts on scepticism, on language and meaning, on types of analysis – idealist, materialist, realist, phenomenological – and so on. If you then wander over to the shelves on literature, you will find a separate section on literary theory (in addition to a section on literary criticism). Here are texts on Marxist and feminist readings, on Freudian and post-Freudian analyses; on deconstructionism, critical theory, reception theory and inter-textuality; on poetics, narratology, rhetoric, allegory and so forth. But then continue over to the history area. Here it is almost certain that there will be no section on history theory (even the phrase looks odd and clumsy – befitting unfamiliarity) but only, tucked away discreetly amongst the serried ranks of history books, the aforementioned Elton and others with, if you are lucky, perhaps an odd copy of (a now domesticated) Geyl or Bloch or Collingwood or, if you are luckier still, a 'recent' Hayden White or a Foucault.[5] In other words, in moving across a few feet of flooring you are, in the main, moving across a generation gap; from theoretically rich and very recent texts to works on the nature of history produced twenty to thirty years ago or, in the case of Bloch and his contemporaries, in the 1930s and 1940s.

Now this is obviously not to say that enormously sophisticated and more recent texts on history and 'history theory' do not exist (thus, variously, Callinicos or Oakeshott; thus various post-modernist works; thus developments in the areas of intellectual and cultural history[6]). Nor is it to say that this lack of concern for history theory and its consequences has not been regularly noticed. Long ago Gareth Stedman-Jones pointed to the poverty of English empiricism; more recently Raphael Samuel has commented on the relatively retarded condition of much historical work with its fetishism of the document, its obsession with 'the facts' and its accompanying methodolgy of 'naïve realism'. David Cannadine's essay, with his strictures against the sterility, downright dullness and myopia of much mainstream history, has been much referred to by professional historians, whilst Christopher Parker's study of the major characteristics of the 'English tradition' of historical writing as exemplified by its leading exponents since *c.* 1850, is an investigation of that deep rut within which a certain type of individualism has run, a methodological perspective largely unreflexive about its own ideological presuppositions.[7] Yet such developments and analyses as these have not significantly fed through so as to inform the more popular surveys and guides to the nature of history. Theoretical discussions are still on the whole skirted by robustly practical practising historians, and certainly the occasional text on theory does not exert the same kind of heavy pressure that the many texts on, say, literary theory, exert on the study of literature.

But arguably this is the way that history ought to go if it is to be 'modernised'. Accordingly I have drawn here on such related areas as philosophy and literary theory. For if 'doing history' is about how you can read and make sense of the past and the present, then it seems important to me to use discourses that have 'readings' and the construction of meanings as major concerns.[8]

How, then, is the text structured? It has three quite deliberately short chapters.[9] In the first I address directly the question of what history is and how the history question can be answered in ways which do not necessarily replicate more 'English' formulations, that do not leave such dominant (common-sense) discourses as unproblematic and which begin to open up history to somewhat wider perspectives. (Bear in mind that 'history' is really 'histories', for at this point we ought to stop thinking of history as though it were a simple and rather obvious thing and recognise that there is a multiplicity of types of history whose only common feature is that their ostensible object of enquiry is 'the past'.)

In chapter 2 I apply that definition to some of the issues and problems commonly surfacing in some of the more basic and introductory debates about the nature of history. Here I shall argue that, although regularly posed, such issues and problems are more rarely resolved or put into context, leaving them tantalisingly open ended and/or mystifying. These are problems such as: is it possible to say what really happened in the past, to get to the truth, to reach objective understandings or, if not, is history incorrigibly interpretive? What are historical facts (and indeed are there any such things)? What is bias and what does it mean to say that historians ought to detect it and root it out? Is it possible to empathise with people who lived in the past? Is a scientific history possible or is history essentially an art? What is the status of those couplets that so often appear in definitions of what history is all about: cause and effect, similarity and difference, continuity and change?

In chapter 3 I pull together all the points I will by then have made by relating them to the position from which I am working; by inserting them into the context that I think informs this text. I have said already that the point of the text is to offer some assistance towards the working out of some of the arguments that gravitate around the question of what is history and so, to further this aim, I thought it appropriate to say why I consider what history is in the way that I do and not in other ways, to position myself in the discourse I have been commenting upon and consider its possibilities. I hasten to add that I do this not because my ideas are necessarily of much significance but because, not existing in a vacuum, it may well be that the times that have produced me, that have so to speak 'written me', will already have and will continue to write you too. I refer to these times as post-modern and thus end with a short contextualising chapter entitled 'Doing history in the post-modern world' – arguably the world we live in.

Chapter 1

What history is

In this chapter I want to try and answer the question 'what is history?' To do this I will look initially at what history is in theory; secondly examine what it is in practice; and finally put theory and practice together into a definition – a methodologically informed sceptical/ironic definition – that I hope is comprehensive enough to give you a reasonable grip not only on the 'history question' but also on some of the debates and positions that surround it.

ON THEORY

At the level of theory I would like to make two points. The first (which I will outline in this paragraph and then develop) is that history is one of a series of discourses about the world. These discourses do not create the world (that physical stuff on which we apparently live) but they do appropriate it and give it all the meanings it has. That bit of the world which is history's (ostensible) object of enquiry is the past. History as discourse is thus in a different category to that which it discourses about, that is, the past and history are different things. Additionally, the past and history are not stitched into each other such that only one historical reading of the past is absolutely necessary. The past and history float free of each other, they are ages and miles apart. For the same object of enquiry can be read differently by different discursive practices (a landscape can be read/interpreted differently by geographers, sociologists, historians, artists, economists, etc.) whilst, internal to each, there are different interpretive readings over time and space; as far as history is concerned historiography shows this.

The above paragraph is not an easy one. I have made a lot of statements, but all of them revolve, actually, around the distinction between the past and history. This distinction is therefore crucial for you to understand, for if it is appreciated then it and the debates it gives rise to will help to clarify what history is in theory. Accordingly I will examine the points I have just made, by looking in some detail at the past–history difference and then by considering some of the main consequences arising from it.

Let me begin with the idea that history is a discourse about, but categorically different from, the past. This might strike you as odd for you may have missed this distinction before or, if not, you may still not have bothered too much about it. One of the reasons why this is so, why the distinction is generally left unworked, is because as English-speakers we tend to lose sight of the fact that there actually is this distinction between history – as that which has been written/recorded about the past – and the past itself, because the word history covers both things.[1] It would be preferable, therefore, always to register this difference by using the term 'the past' for all that has gone on before everywhere, whilst using the word 'historiography' for history, historiography referring here to the writings of historians. This would be good practice (the past as the object of the historians' attention, historiography as the way historians attend to it) leaving the word 'History' (with a capital H) to refer to the whole ensemble of relations. However, habit might be hard to break, and I might myself use the word 'history' to refer to the past, to historiography and to the totality of relationships. But remember if and when I do, I keep the said distinction in mind – and you should too.

It may well be, however, that this clarification on the past–history distinction seems inconsequential; that one is left thinking, so what? What does it matter? Let me offer three illustrations of why the past–history distinction is important to understand.

1 The past has occurred. It has gone and can only be brought back again by historians in very different media, for example in books, articles, documentaries, etc., not as actual events. The past has gone and history is what historians make of it when they go to work. History is the labour of historians (and/or

those acting as if they were historians) and when they meet, one of the first questions they ask each other is what they are working on. It is this work, embodied in books, periodicals, etc., that you read when you do history ('I am going to university to read history'). What this means is that history is quite literally on library and other shelves. Thus if you start a course on seventeenth-century Spain, you do not actually go to the seventeenth century or to Spain; you go, with the help of your reading list, to the library. This is where seventeenth-century Spain is – between Dewey numbers – for where else do teachers send you in order to 'read it up'? Of course you could go to other places where you can find other traces of the past – for example Spanish archives – but wherever you go, when you get there you will have 'to read'. This reading is not spontaneous or natural but learned – on various courses for example – and informed (made meaning-full) by other texts. History (historiography) is an inter-textual, linguistic construct.

2 Let us say that you have been studying part of England's past – the sixteenth century – at A level. Let us imagine that you have used one major text-book: Elton's *England under the Tudors*. In class you have discussed aspects of the sixteenth century, you have class notes, but for your essays and the bulk of your revision you have used Elton. When the exam came along you wrote in the shadow of Elton. And when you passed, you gained an A level in English history, a qualification for considering aspects of 'the past'. But really it would be more accurate to say you have an A level in Geoffrey Elton: for what, actually, at this stage, is your 'reading' of the English past if not basically his reading of it?

3 These two brief examples of the past–history distinction may seem innocuous, but actually it can have enormous effects. For example, although millions of women have lived in the past (in Greece, Rome, the Middle Ages, Africa, America . . .) few of them appear in history, that is, in history texts. Women, to use a phrase, have been 'hidden from history', that is, systematically excluded from most historians' accounts. Accordingly, feminists are now engaged in the task of 'writing women back into history', whilst both men and women are looking at the interconnected constructions of masculinity.[2] And at this point you might pause to consider how many other groups,

people(s), classes, have been/are omitted from histories and why; and what might be the consequences if such omitted 'groups' were central to historical accounts and the now central groups were marginalised.

More will be said about the significance and possibilities of working the past–history distinction later, but I would now like to look at another argument from the earlier paragraph (p. 5) where I said that we have to understand that the past and history are not stitched into each other such that one and only one reading of any phenomenon is entailed, that the same object of enquiry is capable of being read differently by different discourses whilst, internal to each, there are different readings over space and time.

To begin to illustrate this, let us imagine that through a window we can see a landscape (though not all of it because the window-frame quite literally 'frames' it). We can see in the foreground several roads; beyond we can see other roads with houses along-side; we can see rolling fields with farmhouses in them; on the skyline, some miles away, we can see ridges of hills. In the middle distance we can see a market-town. The sky is a watery blue.

Now there is nothing in this landscape that says 'geography'. Yet clearly a geographer could account for it geographically. Thus s/he might read the land as displaying specific field patterns and farming practices; the roads could become part of a series of local/regional communication networks, the farms and town could be read in terms of a specific population distribution; contour maps could chart the terrain, climatic geographers could explain the climate/weather and, say, consequent types of irrigation. In this way the view could become something else – geography. Similarly, a sociologist could take the same landscape and construct it sociologically: people in the town could become data for occupational structures, size of family units, etc.; population distribution could be considered in terms of class, income, age, sex; climate could be seen as affecting leisure facilities, and so on.

Historians too can turn the same landscape into their discourse. Field patterns today could be compared to those pre-enclosure; population now to that of 1831, 1871; land ownership and political power analysed over time; one could examine how a bit of the view edges into a national park, of when and why the railway and canal ceased functioning and so on.

Now, given that there is nothing intrinsic in the view that shouts geography, sociology, history, etc., then we can see clearly that whilst historians and the rest of them do not invent the view (all that stuff seems to be there all right) they do invent all its descriptive categories and any meanings it can be said to have. They construct the analytical and methodological tools to make out of this raw material their ways of reading and talking about it: discoursing. In that sense we read the world as a text, and, logically, such readings are infinite. By which I do not mean that we just make up stories about the world/the past (that is, that we know the world/the past and then make up stories about them) but rather the claim is a much stronger one; that the world/the past comes to us always already as stories and that we cannot get out of these stories (narratives) to check if they correspond to the real world/past, because these 'always already' narratives constitute 'reality'. Which means, in the example being discussed, that the landscape (which only becomes meaningful as a reading) cannot fix such readings once and for all; thus geographers may interpret and re-interpret (read and re-read) the landscape endlessly whilst arguing about just what is being said here 'geographically'. Additionally, given that geography as a discourse has not always existed, then not only have geographers' readings had to begin and not only have they differed over space and time, but geographers have themselves understood/read what constitutes the discourse they are working within differently too; that is, geography itself as a way of reading the world needs interpreting/historicising. And so it is with sociology and history. Different sociologists and historians interpret the same phenomenon differently through discourses that are always on the move, that are always being de-composed and re-composed; are always positioned and positioning, and which thus need constant self-examination as discourses by those who use them.

At this point, then, let me assume that the argument that history as a discourse is categorically different to the past has been indicated. I said at the start of the chapter, however, that at the level of theory *vis-à-vis* what is history, I would be making two points. Here is the second.

Given the past–history distinction, the problem for the historian who somehow wants to capture the past within his/her history thus becomes: how do you fit these two things together? Obviously how this connection is attempted, how the historian tries to know the past, is crucial in determining the possibilities of what history is and can be, not least because it is history's claim to knowledge (rather than belief or assertion) that makes it the discourse it is (I mean, historians do not usually see themselves as writers of fiction, although inadvertently they may be).[3] Yet because of the past–history difference, and because the object of enquiry that historians work on is, in most of its manifestations, actually absent in that only traces of the past remain, then clearly there are all kinds of limits controlling the knowledge claims that historians can make. And for me, in this fitting together of past–history, there are three very problematic theoretical areas: areas of epistemology, methodology and ideology, each of which must be discussed if we are to see what history is.

Epistemology (from the Greek *episteme* = knowledge) refers to the philosophical area of theories of knowledge. This area is concerned with how we know about anything. In that sense history is part of another discourse, philosophy, taking part in the general question of what it is possible to know with reference to its own area of knowledge – the past. And here you might see the problem already, for if it is hard to know about something that exists, to say something about an effectively absent subject like 'the past in history' is especially difficult. It seems obvious that all such knowledge is therefore likely to be tentative, and constructed by historians working under all kinds of presuppositions and pressures which did not, of course, operate on people in the past. Yet, we still see historians trying to raise before us the spectre of the real past, an objective past about which their accounts are accurate and even true. Now I think such certaintist claims are not – and never were – possible to achieve, and I would say that in our current situation this ought to be obvious – as I will argue in chapter 3. Yet to accept this, to allow doubt to run, clearly affects what you might think history is, that is, it gives you part of the answer to what history is and can be. For to admit not really to know, to see history as being (logically) anything you want it to be (the fact–value distinction allows this; besides there have been so very many histories) poses the question of how specific histories came to be constructed into one shape rather than another, not only epistemologically, but methodologically and ideologically too. Here, what can be known and how we can know interact with power. Yet in a sense this is so – and this point must be stressed – only because of history's epistemological fragility. For if it were possible to know once and for all, now and for ever, then there would be no need for any more history to be written, for what would be the point of countless historians saying it all over again in the same way? History (historical constructions not 'the past/future') would stop, and if you think that the idea of stopping history (historians) is absurd it really isn't: stopping history is not only part of Orwell's *1984* for example, but a part of European experience in the 1930s – the more immediate time and place that made Orwell consider it.

Epistemological fragility, then, allows for historians' readings to be multifarious (one past – many histories) so what is it that makes history so epistemologically fragile? There are four basic reasons.

First (and in what follows I draw on David Lowenthal's arguments in his *The Past is a Foreign Country*[4]) no historian can cover and thus re-cover the totality of past events because their 'content' is virtually limitless. One cannot recount more than a fraction of what has occurred and no historian's account ever corresponds precisely with the past: the sheer bulk of the past precludes total history. Most information about the past has never been recorded and most of the rest was evanescent.

Second, no account can re-cover the past as it was because the past was not an account but events, situations, etc. As the past has gone, no account can ever be checked against it but only against other accounts. We judge the 'accuracy' of historians' accounts *vis-à-vis* other historians' interpretations and there is no real account, no proper history that, deep down, allows us to check all other accounts against it: there is no fundamentally correct 'text' of which other interpretations are just variations; variations are all there are. Here the cultural critic Steven Giles is succinct when he comments that what has gone before is *always* apprehended through the sedimented layers of previous interpretations and through the reading habits and categories developed by previous/current interpretive discourses.[5] And this insight allows us to make the point that this way of seeing things makes the study of history (the past) necessarily a study of historiography (historians), historiography therefore being considered not as an extra to the study of history but as actually constituting it. This is an area I shall return to in chapter 2; but now to the third point.

And this is that no matter how verifiable, how widely acceptable or checkable, history remains inevitably a personal construct, a manifestation of the historian's perspective as a 'narrator'. Unlike direct memory (itself suspect) history relies on someone else's eyes and voice; we see through an interpreter who stands between past events and our readings of them. Of course, as Lowenthal says, written history 'in practice' cuts down the historian's logical freedom to write anything by allowing the reader access to his/her sources, but the historian's viewpoint and predilections still shape the choice of historical materials, and our own personal constructs determine what we make of them. The past that we 'know' is always contingent upon our own views, our own 'present'. Just as we are ourselves products of the past so the known past (history) is an artefact of ours. Nobody, however immersed in the past, can divest himself/herself of his/her own knowledge and assumptions. To explain the past, Lowenthal notes, 'historians go beyond the actual record to frame hypotheses in present day modes of thought . . . "we are moderns and our words and thought can not but be modern", noted Maitland, "it is too late for us to be early English".'[6] There are, then, few limits to the shaping power of interpretive, imagining words. 'Look' says the poet Khlebnikov in his *Decrees To The Planets*, 'the sun obeys my syntax.'[7] 'Look', says the historian, 'the past obeys my interpretation.'

Now this might look slightly poetical itself, so the point being made about sources at one and the same time preventing the historian's total freedom and yet not fixing things such that they can really stop endless interpretations might be illustrated by a mundane example. Thus there are many disagreements as to Hitler's intentions after gaining power, and the causes of the Second World War. One such famous long-running disagreement has been between A. J. P. Taylor and H. Trevor-Roper. This disagreement was not based on their merits as historians; both are very experienced, both have 'skills', both can read documents and in this case they often read the same ones, yet still they disagreed. Thus whilst the sources may prevent just anything at all from being said, nevertheless the same events/sources do not entail that one and only one reading has to follow.

The above three reasons for epistemological fragility are based on the idea that history is less than the past; that historians can only recover fragments. But the fourth point stresses that, through hindsight, we in a way know more about the past than the people who lived in it. In translating the past into modern terms and in using knowledge perhaps previously unavailable, the historian discovers both what has been forgotten about the past and pieces together things never pieced together before. People and social formations are thus caught up in processes that can only be seen in retrospect, and documents and other traces are ripped out of their original contexts of purpose and function to illustrate, say, a pattern which might not be remotely meaningful to any of their authors. And all this is, as Lowenthal says, inevitable. History always conflates, it changes, it exaggerates aspects of the past: 'Time is foreshortened, details selected and highlighted, action concentrated, relations simplified, not to [deliberately] alter ... the events but to ... give them meaning.'[8] Even the most empirical chronicler has to invent narrative structures to give shape to time and place: 'Res gestae may well be one damned thing after another ... but it cannot possibly appear as such for all meaning would then be extruded from it.'[9] And because stories emphasise linkages and play down the role of breaks, of ruptures, then, concludes Lowenthal, histories as known to us appear more comprehensible than we have any reason to believe the past was.

These then are the main (and well known) epistemological limits. I have drawn them quickly and impressionistically and you might go on to read Lowenthal and the others yourself. But I now intend to move on. For if these are the epistemological limits to what can be known, then they obviously interconnect with the ways historians try and find out as much as they can. And, with historians' methods as with epistemology, there are no definitive ways that have to be used by virtue of their being correct; historians' methods are every bit as fragile as their epistemologies.

So far I have argued that history is a shifting discourse constructed by historians and that from the existence of the past no one reading is entailed: change the gaze, shift the perspective and new readings appear. Yet although historians know all this, most seem to studiously ignore it and strive for objectivity and truth nevertheless. And this striving for truth cuts through ideological/methodological positions.

Thus on the empirical right (somewhat), G. Elton in *The Practice of History*[10] states at the start of his chapter on research: 'The study of history, then, amounts to a search for the truth.' And, although the same chapter ends with a series of qualifications – 'He [the historian] knows that what he is studying is real [but] he knows that he can never recover all of it . . . he knows that the process of historical research and reconstruction will never end, but he is also conscious that this does not render his work unreal or illegitimate' – it is obvious that such caveats do not seriously affect Elton's originally stated 'truth search'.

On the Marxist left (somewhat), E. P. Thompson in *The Poverty of Theory*[11] writes that, 'For some time . . . the materialist conception of history . . . has been growing in self-confidence. As a mature practice . . . it is perhaps the strongest discipline deriving from the Marxist tradition. Even in my own life-time . . . the advances have been considerable, and one had supposed these to be advances in *knowledge*.' Thompson admits that this is not to say that such knowledge is subject to 'scientific proof', but he holds it to be real knowledge nevertheless.

In the empirical centre (somewhat), A. Marwick in *The Nature of History*[12] appreciates what he calls the 'subjective dimension' of historians' accounts, but for him this doesn't live in, say, the historian's ideological position, but in the nature of the evidence, historians being 'forced into a greater display of personal interpretation by the imperfections of their source materials'. This being the case Marwick thus argues that it is the job of historians to develop 'tight methodological rules' whereby they can reduce their 'moral' interventions by 'bowing down' before the evidence so allowing the past to speak 'directly'. Thus Marwick links up to Elton: 'Elton is keen to establish that just because historical explanation does not depend upon universal laws, that does not mean it is not governed by very strict rules.' And so, for all these historians, truth, knowledge and legitimacy derive from tight methodological rules and procedures. It is this that cuts down interpretive flux.

My argument is different. For me what determines interpretation ultimately lies beyond method and evidence in ideology. For while most historians would agree that a rigorous method is important, there is a problem as to which rigorous method they are talking about. In Marwick's own section on method he reviews a selection from which one can (presumably) chose. Thus, would you like to follow Hegel or Marx or Dilthey or Weber or Popper or Hempel or Aron or Collingwood or Dray or Oakeshott or Danto or Gallie or Walsh or Atkinson or Leff or Hexter? Would you care to go along with modern empiricists, feminists, the Annales School, neo-Marxists, new-stylists, econometricians, structuralists or post-structuralists, or even Marwick himself, to name but twenty-five possibilities? And this is a short list! The point is that even if you could make a choice, what would be the criteria? How could one know which method would lead to the 'truer' past? Of course each method would be rigorous, that is, internally coherent and consistent, but it would also be self-referencing. That is, it might tell you how to conduct valid arguments within itself but, given that all the choices do this, then the problem of discriminating somehow between twenty-five alternatives just will not go away. Thompson is rigorous and so is Elton; on what grounds does one choose? On Marwick's? But why his? So, is it not likely that in the end one chooses say, Thompson, because one just likes what Thompson does with his method; one likes his reasons for doing history: for all other things being equal, why else might one take up a position?

To summarise. Talk of method as the road to truth is misleading. There is a range of methods without any agreed criteria for choosing. Often people like Marwick argue that despite all the methodological differences between, say, empiricists and structuralists, they do nevertheless agree on the fundamentals. But this again is not so. The fact that structuralists go to enormous lengths to explain very precisely that they are not empiricists; the fact that they invented their specific approaches precisely to differentiate themselves from everyone else seems to have been a point somewhat ignored by Marwick and the others.

I want now to deal briefly with just one further argument regarding method which regularly occurs in introductory debates about the 'nature of history'. It is about concepts and it runs as follows: it may well be that the differences between methods cannot be closed down, but are there not key concepts that all historians use? Doesn't this imply some common methodological ground?

Now it is certainly the case that, in all types of histories, one constantly meets so called 'historical concepts' (by not calling them 'historians' concepts' such concepts look impersonal and objective, as though they belong to a history that is somehow self-generating). Not only that, such concepts are referred to quite regularly as the 'heartlands' of history. These are concepts such as time, evidence, empathy, cause and effect, continuity and change, and so on.

I am not going to argue that you should not 'work' concepts, but I am concerned that when presenting these particular ones, the impression is strongly given that they are indeed obvious and timeless and that they do constitute the universal building blocks of historical knowledge. Yet this is ironic, for one of the things that the opening up of history ought to have done is to historicise history itself; to see all historical accounts as imprisoned in time and space and thus to see their concepts not as universal heartlands but as specific, local expressions. This historicisation is easy to demonstrate in the case of 'common' concepts.

In an article on new developments in history, the educationalist Donald Steel has considered how certain concepts became 'heartland concepts', showing how in the 1960s five major concepts were identified as constituting history: time, space, sequence, moral judgement and social realism.[13] Steel points out that these were refined (not least by himself) by 1970 to provide the 'key concepts' of history: time, evidence, cause and effect, continuity and change, and similarity and difference. Steel explains that it was these that became the basis for School's Council History, the GCSE, certain A level developments, and which have been influential both in undergraduate courses and more generally. Apparently then these 'old' heartlands have been pumping away for less than twenty years, are not universal, and do not come out of historians' methods as such but very much out of general educational thinking. Obviously they are ideological too, for what might happen if other concepts were used to organise the (dominant) field: structure–agency, overdetermination, conjuncture, uneven development, centre–periphery, dominant–marginal, base–superstructure, rupture, genealogy, *mentalité*, hegemony, élite, paradigm, etc.? It is time to address ideology directly.

Let me begin with an example. It would be possible at this point in space and time to place in any school or undergraduate history syllabus a course that would be quite properly historical (in that it looked like other histories) but in which the choice of subject matter and the methodological approach was made from a black, Marxist, feminist perspective. Yet I doubt if any such course could be found. Why not? Not because it would not be history, for it would, but because black Marxist-feminists don't really have the power to put such a course into this sort of public circulation. Yet if one were to ask those who might well have the power to decide what does constitute 'suitable courses', who might well have the power to effect such inclusions/exclusions, then it is likely that they would argue that the reason for such a non-appearance is because such a course would be ideological – that is, that the motives for such a history would come from concerns external to history *per se*; that it would be a vehicle for the delivery of a specific position for persuasive purposes. Now this distinction between 'history as such' and 'ideological history' is interesting because it implies, and is meant to imply, that certain histories (generally the dominant ones) are not ideological at all, do not position people, and do not deliver views of the past that come from outside 'the subject'. But we have already seen that meanings given to histories of all descriptions are necessarily that; not meanings intrinsic in the past (any more than the 'land-scape' had our meanings already in its before we put them there) but meanings given to the past from outside(rs). History is never for itself; it is always for someone.

Accordingly it seems plausible to say that particular social formations want their historians to deliver particular things. It also seems plausible to say that the predominantly delivered positions will be in the interests of those stronger ruling blocs within social formations, not that such positions are automatically achieved, unchallenged or secured once and for all and 'that is it'. The fact that history *per se* is an ideological construct means that it is constantly being re-worked and re-ordered by all those who are variously affected by power relationships; because the dominated as well as the dominant also have their versions of the past to legitimate their practices, versions which have to be

excluded as improper from any place on the agenda of the dominant discourse. In that sense re-orderings of the messages to be
delivered (often many such re-orderings are referred to academically as 'controversies') just have to be constructed continuously
because the needs of the dominant/subordinate are constantly
being re-worked in the real world as they seek to mobilise
people(s) in support of their interests. History is forged in such
conflict and clearly these conflicting needs for history impinge
upon the debates (struggle for ownership) as to what history is.

So, at this point, can we not see that the way to answer the
question of 'what is history?' in ways that are realistic is to
substitute the word 'who' for 'what', and add 'for' to the end of
the phrase; thus, the question becomes not 'what is history?' but
'who is history for?' If we do this then we can see that history is
bound to be problematic because it is a contested term/discourse,
meaning different things to different groups. For some groups
want a sanitised history where conflict and distress are absent;
some want history to lead to quietism; some want history to
embody rugged individualism, some to provide strategies and
tactics for revolution, some to provide grounds for counter-revol-
ution, and so on. It is easy to see how history for a revolutionary is
bound to be different from that desired by a conservative. It is
also easy to see how the list of uses for history is not only logically
but practically endless; I mean, what would a history be like that
everyone could once and for all agree on? Let me briefly clarify
these comments with an illustration.

In his novel *1984*, Orwell wrote that those who control the
present control the past and those who control the past control
the future. This seems likely outside fiction too. Thus people(s) in
the present need antecedents to locate themselves now and legitimate their ongoing and future ways of living. (Actually of course
the 'facts' of the past – or anything else – legitimate nothing at all
given the fact–value distinction, but the point being addressed
here is how people act as if they do.) Thus people(s) literally feel
the need to root themselves today and tomorrow in their yesterdays. Recently such yesterdays have been sought for (and found,
given that the past can and will sustain countless narratives) by
women, blacks, regional groupings, various minorities, etc. In
these pasts explanations for current existences and future programmes are made. A little further back and the working classes

too sought to root themselves by way of a historically contrived trajectory. Further back still the bourgeoisie found its genealogy and began to construct its history for itself (and others). In that sense all classes/groups write their collective autobiographies. History is the way people(s) create, in part, their identities. It is far more than a slot in the school/academic curriculum, though we can see how what goes into such spaces is crucially important for all those variously interested parties.

Do we not know this all the time? Is it not obvious that such an important 'legitimating' phenomenon as history is rooted in real needs and power? I think it is, except that when the dominant discourse refers to the constant re-writing of histories it does so in ways that displace such needs: it muses blandly that each generation re-writes its own history. But the question is how and why? And the arguable answer, alluded to in Orwell, is because power relations produce ideological discourses such as 'history as knowledge' which are necessary for all involved in terms of conflicting legitimation exercises.

Let us conclude the discussion of what history is in theory. I have argued that history is composed of epistemology, methodology and ideology. Epistemology shows we can never really know the past; that the gap between the past and history (historiography) is an ontological one, that is, is in the very nature of things such that no amount of epistemological effort can bridge it. Historians have devised ways of working to cut down the influence of the interpreting historian by developing rigorous methods which they have then tried variously to universalise, so that if everyone practised them then a heartland of skills, concepts, routines and procedures could reach towards objectivity. But there are many methodologies; the so-called heartland concepts are of recent and partial construction, and I have argued that the differences that we see are there because history is basically a contested discourse, an embattled terrain wherein people(s), classes and groups autobiographically construct interpretations of the past literally to please themselves. There is no definitive history outside these pressures, any (temporary) consensus only being reached when dominant voices can silence others either by overt power or covert incorporation. In the end history is theory and theory is ideological and ideology just is material interests. Ideology seeps into every nook and cranny of history, including the everyday practices of making histories in those institutions predominantly set aside in our social formation for that purpose – especially universities. Let us now look at history as that sort of practice.

ON PRACTICE

I have just concluded that history has been and will be made for many different reasons and in many places, and that one such type is professional history, that is, the history produced by (generally) salaried historians working (on the whole) in higher education and especially universities. In *The Death of the Past*[14] the historian J. H. Plumb described such (Elton-like) professional history as the process of trying to establish the truth of what happened in the past and which could then be pitched over against popular memory/common-sense/recipe-knowledge 'pasts' in order to get such half-formed, half-digested (and for Plumb) half-baked constructions out of the way. In *On Living in an Old Country*,[15] Patrick Wright has argued that not only is Plumb's task impossible because, as we have seen, there are no unproblematic historical (historians') truths as such; and that not only is Plumb's aim possibly undesirable because in, say, popular memory, there may well lie strengths and alternative readings which it might be necessary to oppose at times to 'official' histories (Wright suggests we think here of the proles' memories in Orwell's *1984*) but also because one type of institution where such eradication might be carried out, the educational institution, is itself intimately involved in popular memory-type socialisation processes. For although professional historians overwhelmingly present themselves as academic and disinterested, and although they are certainly in some ways 'distanced', nevertheless, it is more illuminating to see such practitioners as being not so much outside the ideological fray but as occupying very dominant positions within it; to see professional histories as expressions of how dominant ideologies currently articulate history 'academically'. It seems rather obvious that, seen in a wider cultural and 'historical' perspective, multi-million pound institutional investments such as our national universities are integral to the reproduction of the on-going social formation and are thus at the forefront of cultural guardianship (academic standards) and ideological control; it would be somewhat careless if they were not.

Given that I have tried so far to locate history in the interstices of real interests and pressures, I need to consider 'scholarly' pressures too, not only because it is their type of history that predominantly defines the field as to what 'history really is', but also because it is the type of history studied on A level and undergraduate courses. On such courses you are, in effect, being inducted into academic history; you are to become like the professionals. So what are the professionals like and how do they make histories?[16]

Let us start this way. History is produced by a group of labourers called historians when they go to work; it is their job. And when they go to work they take with them certain identifiable things.

First they take themselves personally: their values, positions, their ideological perspectives.

Second they take their epistemological presuppositions. These are not always held very consciously but historians will have 'in mind' ways of gaining 'knowledge'. Here will come into play a range of categories – economic, social, political, cultural, ideological, etc. – a range of concepts across/within these categories (thus within the political category there may be much use of, say, class, power, state, sovereignty, legitimacy, etc.) and broad assumptions about the constancy, or otherwise, of human beings (ironically and a-historically referred to very often as 'human nature'). Through the use of these categories, concepts and assumptions, the historian will generate hypotheses, formulate abstractions, and organise and reorganise his/her materials to include and exclude. Historians also use technical vocabularies and these in turn (aside from being inevitably anachronistic) affect not only what they say but the way they say it. Such categories, concepts and vocabularies are constantly being reworked, but without them historians would not be able to understand each others' accounts or make up their own, no matter how much they may disagree about things.

Third, historians have routines and procedures (methods, in the narrow sense of the term) for close working on material: ways of checking it for its origins, position, authenticity, reliability. . . . These routines will apply to all the materials worked on albeit with various degrees of concentration and rigour (many slips and mis-takes occur). Here are a range of techniques running from the elaborate to the nitty-gritty; these are the sorts of practices often referred to as 'historians' *skills*', techniques which we can see now, in passing, as but themselves passing moments in that combination of factors that make histories. (In other words history is not about 'skills'.) So, armed with these sorts of practices, the historian can get down more directly to 'make up' some history – 'making histories'.

Fourth, in going about their work of finding various materials to work on and 'work up', historians shuttle between other historians' published work(s) (stored up labour-time as embodied in books, articles, etc.) and unpublished materials. This unpublished 'newish' material can be called the traces of the past (literally the remaining marks from the past – documents, records, artefacts, etc.), these traces being a mixture of the known (but little used) trace, new, unused and possibly unknown traces, and old traces; that is, materials used before but, because of the newish/new traces found, now capable of being placed in contexts different to those they have occupied before. The historian can then begin to organise all these elements in new (and various) ways – always looking for that longed-for 'original thesis' – and so begins to transform the traces of the once concrete into the 'concrete in thought', that is, into historians' accounts. Here the historian literally re-produces the traces of the past in a new category and this act of trans-formation – the past into history – is his/her basic job.

Fifth, having done their research, historians then have to write it up. This is where the epistemological, methodological and ideological factors again come into play, interconnecting with everyday practices, as they will have done throughout the research phases. Obviously such pressures of the everyday will vary but some include:

1 Pressures from family and/or friends ('Not another weekend working!' 'Can't you give your work a rest?');
2 Pressures from the work-place, where the various influences of heads of faculty, departmental heads, peer group, institutional research policies and, dare it be said, the obligation to teach students, all bear down;

3 Pressures from publishers with regard to several factors:

wordage: the constraints on wordage are considerable and have effects. Think how different historical knowledge could be were all books a third shorter or four times longer than 'normal' size!

format: the size of page, print, with or without illustrations, with or without exercises, bibliography, index, etc.; in loose-leaf, with accompanying tape or video – all these have effects too.

market: who the historian sees as his/her market will influence what is said and how: think how the French Revolution of 1789 would have to be 'different' for young school children, sixth-formers, non-Europeans, 'revolutionary specialists', the interested layman.

deadlines: how long the writer has in total to do the research and write it up, and how that time is allocated (one day a week, a term off, at weekends) affects, say, the availability of sources, the historian's concentration, etc. Again, the sorts of conditions the publisher sets regarding completion are often crucial.

literary style: how the historian writes (polemically, discur-sively, flamboyantly, pedantically, and in combinations of these) and the grammatical, syntactical and semantic reach, all affect the account and may well have to be modified to fit the publisher's house-style, series format, etc.

referees: publishers send manuscripts to readers who may call for drastic changes in terms of the organisation of material (this text, for example, was originally nearly twice as long); again, some referees have been known to have axes to grind.

re-writing: at all stages until the text goes to print re-writings take place. Sometimes sections will require three drafts, sometimes thirteen. Bright ideas that seemed initially to say it all become weary and flat when you have tried to write it all a dozen times; again, things you were originally putting in are left out and things left in often seem hostages to fortune. What kinds of judgements are involved here as the writer 'works' all those traces read and noted (often imperfectly) so long before?

And so on. Now, these are obvious points (think here how

many outside factors, that is, factors outside 'the past', operate on you and influence what you write in essays and studies), but the thing to stress here is that none of these pressures, indeed none of the processes discussed in this chapter, operated on the events being accounted for; on, say, manpower planning in the First World War. Here, again, the gaps between the past and history yawn.

Sixth, what has been written so far has been about the production of histories. But texts also have to be read; consumed. Just as you can consume cake, in many different ways (slowly, gulping it), in a variety of situations (at work, driving a car), in relation to other courses (have you already had enough, is digestion hard) and in a variety of settings (if you're on a diet, at a wedding), none of which ever comes round in exactly the same way again, so the consumption of a text takes place in contexts that do not repeat themselves. Quite literally no two readings are the same. (Sometimes you might write comments in the margins of a text and then, returning to it some time later, not remember why you wrote what you did; yet they are exactly the same words on the same page, so just how do meanings retain meaning?) Thus no reading, even by the same person, can be guaranteed to produce the same effects repeatedly, which means that authors cannot force their intentions/interpretations on the reader. Conversely, readers cannot fully fathom everything the authors intend. Further, the same text can be inserted first into one broad discourse and then into another: there are no logical limits, each reading is another writing. This is the world of the deconstructionist text where any text, in other con-texts, can mean many things. Here is a 'world of difference'.

And yet these last remarks seem to raise a problem (but on your reading did a problem arise for you; and is yours different to mine?). The problem raised for me is this: although the above seems to suggest that all is interpretive flux, in fact we 'read' in fairly predictable ways. So, in that sense, what pins readings down? Well, not detailed agreement on all and everything because the details will always float free – specific things can always be made to mean more or less – but general agreements do occur. They do so because of power; here we return to ideology. For what arguably stops texts from being used in totally arbitrary ways is the fact that certain texts are nearer to some texts than others; are more or less locatable into genres, into slots; are more or less congenial to the needs that people(s) have and which are expressed in texts. And so, *après* Orwell, they find affinities and fixing posts (booklists, recommended readings, Dewey numbers) that are themselves ultimately arbitrary, but which relate to the more permanent needs of groups and classes: we live in a social system – not a social random. This is a complicated but essential area to consider and you might note here texts by theorists such as Scholes, Eagleton, Fish and Bennett, wherein how this might well work is discussed.[17] You might also reflect upon how this somewhat baffling situation – of the wayward text which does not logically have to settle down but which does so in practice – relates to an interpretive anxiety which students often have. Their anxiety is this: if you understand that history is what historians make; that they make it on slender evidence; that history is inescapably interpretive and that there are at least half a dozen sides to every argument so that history is relative, then you might think well, if it seems just interpretation and nobody really knows, then why bother doing it? If it is all relative what is the point? This is a state of mind we might call 'hapless relativism'.

In a sense this way of looking at things is a positive one. It is liberating, for it throws out old certainties and those who have benefited from them are capable of being exposed. And in a sense everything is relative (historicist). But, liberating or not, this still sometimes leaves people feeling as if they are in a dead end. Yet there is no need to. To deconstruct other peoples' histories is the precondition of constructing your own in ways which suggest you know what you are doing; in ways which remind you that history is always history for someone. For although, as I have said, logically all accounts are problematic and relative, the point is that some are actually dominant and others marginal. All are logically the same but in actuality they are different; they are in evaluative (albeit ultimately groundless) hierarchies. The question then becomes 'why?' and the answer is because knowledge is related to power and that, within social formations, those with the most power distribute and legitimate 'knowledge' *vis-à-vis* interests as best they can. This is the way out of relativism in theory, by analyses of power in practice, and thus a relativist perspective need not lead to despair but to the beginning of a

general recognition of how things seem to operate. This is eman-
cipating. Reflexively, you too can make histories.

ON A DEFINITION OF HISTORY

I have just argued that history in the main is what historians
make. So why the fuss; isn't this what history is? In a way it is, but
obviously not quite. What historians do in a narrow working
sense is fairly easy to describe; we can draw up a job description.
The problem, however, comes when this activity gets inserted, as
it must, back into the power relations within any social formation
out of which it comes; when different people(s), groups and
classes ask: 'What does history mean for me/us, and how can it be
used or abused?' It is here, in usages and meanings, that history
becomes so problematic; when the question 'What is history?'
becomes, as I have explained, 'Who is history for?' This is the
bottom line; so, what is history for me? A definition:

> History is a shifting, problematic discourse, ostensibly
> about an aspect of the world, the past, that is produced by a
> group of present-minded workers (overwhelmingly in our
> culture salaried historians) who go about their work in
> mutually recognisable ways that are epistemologically,
> methodologically, ideologically and practically positioned
> and whose products, once in circulation, are subject to a
> series of uses and abuses that are logically infinite but which
> in actuality generally correspond to a range of power bases
> that exist at any given moment and which structure and
> distribute the meanings of histories along a dominant–
> marginal spectrum.[18]

Chapter 2

On some questions and some answers

Having given a definition of history I now want to work it such that it might give answers to the sort of basic questions that often arise with regard to the nature of history. Because this text is short my comments will be brief; but brief or not, I hope that the answers I will be suggesting point both in the direction and to the way in which more sophisticated, nuanced and qualified responses can be made. Besides, I think a guide such as this (a sort of 'rough guide to history') is needed, not least because, although questions on the nature of history are regularly raised, the tendency is to leave them open so that you can then 'make up your own mind'. Now I too want that, but I am aware that very often the various 'nature of history' debates are perceived only dimly (I mean there seems so many alternatives to fit in, so many possible orderings of the basic constituents) such that some doubt and confusion can remain. So for a change as it were, here are some questions and some answers.

1 What is the status of truth in the discourses of history?
2 Is there any such thing as an objective history (are there objective 'facts' etc.), or is history just interpretation?
3 What is bias and what are the problems involved in trying to get rid of it?
4 What is empathy; can it be done, how, why, and if it cannot be achieved, why does it seem so important to try?
5 What are the differences between primary and secondary sources (traces) and between 'evidence' and 'sources': what is at stake here?
6 What do you do with those couplets (cause and effect,

continuity and change, similarity and difference) and is it possible to do what you are asked to do through using them?
7 Is history an art or a science?

ON TRUTH

It may look as if I have dealt already with whether we can know
the truth of the past. I have run arguments from Elton and others
where the aim of historical study is to gain real (true) knowledge,
and suggested this is, strictly speaking, unachievable. Again I
have tried to show the epistemological, methodological, ideological and practical reasons why this is so. However, I think that two
remaining areas still need to be explored so that previous points
can be developed: first, if we cannot ultimately know the truths of
the past then why do we keep searching for them and, second,
how does the term 'truth' – irrespective of whether or not there is
any such thing – function in the discourses of history?

So why do we need truth? At one level the answer seems
obvious. For without it certaintist concepts – objectivity, essence,
essential, unbiased, etc. – which fix things and close them down,
would be powerless. Without objectivity how do we discriminate
between rival accounts of the same phenomenon; more mun-
danely, how can we actually decide what were the most important causes of the 1832 Reform Act? These sorts of worries seem to
haunt us.

But why? Beyond the immediately practical, where does this
desire for certainty come from? The reasons are many, ranging
from generalisations about the 'western tradition' to psycho–
social fears of 'loss' before uncertainty. The often-quoted comment by the philosopher A. N. Whitehead, that the dominant
philosophical tradition in the west ('The Western Tradition') is a
series of footnotes to Plato explains much, given Plato's view that
absolute knowledge (of justice, of virtue, of the best polity) in its
pure forms was possible and could be ascertained through philosophical argument (with the implication that it would not be
rational to act non-virtuously if one knew what virtue was; a view
that good/true knowledge ought to entail good/true practice).
Also crucial are Christian arguments that the word of God was
the word of Truth, and that knowing Him was knowing Truth;
that Christianity provides criteria for judging everything and

everyone on the scales of right and wrong. Additionally, constant attempts within western thought in so many of its manifestations (philosophy, theology, aesthetics, etc.) to formulate some connection between word and world through correspondence theories of truth, long kept a destructive scepticism (sophism, nominalism, anti-foundationalism) somewhat at bay. The development of rationality and science and the fact that science really does seem 'to work' are further contributing factors. Add to them that in everyday life truth and its synonyms are in common usage ('tell the truth'; 'did you truly say that?'; 'how can I trust you?'; 'are you absolutely certain?'); add to that one's experiences of education ('who can give me the correct answer?' 'do it again, it's wrong'); add to that all those certaintist ticks and crosses on all those exercise books; and add to that all those textbooks that intimidate us because we cannot see how their 'contents' have been made – in all these ways truth seems naturally at hand.

But in a culture nothing is natural. Today we know of no foundations for Platonic absolutes. Today we live with the idea of God's absence. We have deconstructed and made arbitrary and pragmatic the connections between word and world. We have seen, this century, the incapacity of reason to demonstrably disempower irrationalism. Although physicists and engineers get on with their work and their hypothetico-deductive reasonings, the grounds for their success remain enigmatic: 'Why it should be that the external world, in the naïve, obvious sense, should concur with the regularity-postulates, with the mathematical and rule-bound expectations of investigative rationalism, no one knows.'[1] And we understand, of course, the 'common sense', of persistent habitual homilies, long after the reasons for them have gone: 'We still speak of "sunrise" and "sunset". We do so as if the Copernican model of the solar-system had not replaced, ineradicably, the Ptolemaic. Vacant metaphors, eroded figures of speech, inhabit our vocabulary and grammar. They are caught, tenaciously, in the scaffolding and recesses of our common parlance.'[2]

All this then, if we can still use the word, we *know*. We are (our culture is) a-moral, sceptical, ironic, secular. We are partners with uncertainty; we have disturbed truth, have tracked it down and found it to be a linguistic sign, a concept. Truth is a self-referencing figure of speech, incapable of accessing the phenomenal world: word and world, word and object, remain separate. Let us examine now these points in general terms, and then relate them to that similar separation between the phenomenal past and discursive history and so draw this first question to a close.

In *The Order of Things*, Michel Foucault points to both the absurdity and yet the practicality of correspondences between words and things:

> This book first arose out of a passage in Borges, out of the laughter that shattered, as I read the passage, all the familiar landmarks of thought – *our* thought, the thought that bears the stamp of our age and our geography – breaking up all the ordered surfaces and all the planes with which we are accustomed to tame the wild profusion of existing things and continuing long afterwards to disturb and threaten with collapse our age-old distinction between the Same and the Other. This passage quotes 'a certain Chinese Encyclopaedia' in which it is written that animals are divided into:
> (a) belonging to the Emperor
> (b) embalmed
> (c) tame
> (d) sucking pigs
> (e) sirens
> (f) fabulous
> (g) stray dogs
> (h) included in the present classification
> (i) frenzied
> (j) innumerable
> (k) drawn with a very fine camel-haired brush
> (l) *et cetera*
> (m) having just broken the water pitcher
> (n) that from a long way off look like flies.
> In the wonderment of this taxonomy, the thing we apprehend in one great leap, the thing that . . . is demonstrated as the exotic charm of another system of thought, is the limitation of our own, the stark impossibility of [us] thinking *that*.[3]

Foucault's point is clear. It is the arbitrariness of the definition, one that looks so odd to us but not to the encyclopaedist to whom it literally made sense whilst, of course, any definition we offered would look odd to him/her. What is missing here then is any necessary connection between word and world. Thus the literary and cultural theorist, George Steiner:

> It is this break . . . between word and world which constitutes one of the very few genuine revolutions . . . in Western history. . . . The word *rose* has neither stem nor leaf nor thorn. It is neither pink nor red nor yellow. It exudes no odour. It is, *per se*, a wholly arbitrary marker, an empty sign. Nothing whatever . . . in its phonemic components, etymological history or grammatical functions, has any correspondence whatever to what we believe or imagine to be the object of its purely conventional reference.[4]

This 'break' has been underlined by the American pragmatist Richard Rorty, commenting that about two hundred years ago Europeans realised that truth was always created and never found.[5] Yet, despite the slippage between word and world, and despite the fact that all meanings/truths are created in contingent circumstances, things do, nevertheless, seem to correspond. But why, given that in our sceptical–ironic situation they need not do so? Well, for the reasons I have mentioned: that our culture has a long, dominant tradition wherein truth and certainty have been held to be found and not created – Platonism, Christianity, reason, science, the habits of everyday life; and, as I indicated in the last chapter, because of Orwellian/ideological affinities that still manage to hold off theoretical nihilism by their certaintist practices. For ultimately what has stopped anything being said, and has allowed only specific things to run, is power: truth is dependent on somebody having the power to make it true. This is how the concept of truth is made to function (as I say irrespective of whether such 'truths' are really true or not) as a censor. Here, in *Power/Knowledge*, Foucault makes this point:

> Truth isn't outside power . . . it is produced only by virtue of multiple forms of constraint . . . . Each society has . . . its 'general politics' of truth: that is, the types of discourse which it accepts and makes function as true; the mechanisms and instances which enable one to distinguish true and false statements, the means by which each is sanctioned; the techniques and procedures accorded value in the

acquisition of truth; the status of those who are charged
with saying what counts as true.

   . . . by truth I do not mean 'the ensemble of truths which
are to be discovered and accepted' but rather 'the ensemble
of rules according to which the true and the false are sep-
arated and specific effects of power attached to the true', it
being understood also that it is not a matter . . . 'on behalf' of
the truth, but of a battle about the status of truth and the
economic and political role it plays.

   'Truth' is to be understood as a system of ordered procedures for the production, regulation, distribution, circulation and operation of statements. 'Truth' is linked . . . with
systems of power which produce and sustain it . . . . A
'regime of truth'.[6]

All these arguments are readily applicable to history. History is
a discourse, a language game; within it 'truth' and similar expressions are devices to open, regulate and shut down interpretations. Truth acts as a censor – it draws the line. We know that
such truths are really 'useful fictions' that are in discourse by
virtue of power (somebody has to put and keep them there) and
power uses the term 'truth' to exercise control: regimes of truth.
Truth prevents disorder, and it is this fear of disorder (of the
disorderly) or, to put this positively, it is this fear of freedom (for
the unfree) that connects it functionally to material interests.

ON FACTS AND INTERPRETATION

The question of facts and/versus interpretation is typically formulated thus: are there historical facts that we can definitely know
(for example dates) or is history 'just interpretation'?

Are there 'past things' that seem to be factually correct? In one
sense one can say yes. Thus, we know that the so-called Great
War/First World War happened between 1914 and 1918. We
know that Margaret Thatcher came into power in 1979. If these
are facts then we know facts. However, such facts, though important, are 'true' but trite within the larger issues historians
consider. For historians are not too concerned about discrete facts
(facts as individual facts), for such a concern only touches that
part of historical discourse called its chronicle. No, historians

have ambitions, wishing to discover not only what happened but how and why and what these things meant and mean. This is the task historians have set for themselves (I mean they did not have to raise the stakes so high). So it is never really a matter of the facts *per se* but the weight, position, combination and significance they carry *vis-à-vis* each other in the construction of explanations that is at issue. This is the inevitable interpretive dimension, the problematic, as historians transform the events of the past into patterns of meaning that any literal representation of them as facts could never produce. For although there may be methods of finding out 'what happened' there is no method whatsoever whereby one can definitely say what the 'facts' mean. Here Steiner is again relevant. A text, says Steiner, in as much as its components are

> phonetic, grammatical and lexical . . . can be studied analytically and statistically . . . . But . . . the absolutely decisive failing occurs when such approaches seek to formalise *meaning*, when they proceed upward from the phonetic . . . to the semantic . . . . It is this progression which no analytic-linguistic technique . . . has ever taken convincingly.[7]

Clearly this applies to history as discourse. In that the past is a text (full of 'old' texts) to be read and made meaning-full (remember again the view read as geography), then critiques of the limits of any textuality apply. There is no method of establishing incorrigible meanings; all facts to be meaningful need embedding in interpretive readings that obviously contain them but which do not simply somehow arise from them; to the chagrin of empiricists the fact–value dichotomy allows/demands this.[8]

Working historians clearly ought to recognise these arguments. Often they do not, or, if they do, they rarely work them. Historians often seem to assume that interpretations just do derive from the 'always already there facts', and that what is actually a temporary and local interpretation really is true/accurate as such; that at 'the centre' lie the facts of the matter in some given, uninterpreted way.

Now this may appear a little abstract, so let me show what is at stake here by an example.

In a recent (popular) short article[9] the historian Robert Skidelsky wrote on the very problem we have been discussing. In it he

stressed that most historical facts are not in dispute, that relativism poses no threat to the orderly discussion of a basically
agreed body of knowledge and that over most of 'our' interpretations of the past shared values and views predominate. Skidelsky agreed that interpretive activity goes on but argued that it is
located on the margins where it does not call into question that
shared centre; indeed, it is from such a centre that one adjudi-
cates between rival (marginal) perspectives.

In putting this view so clearly Skidelsky speaks for many historians and what he is saying can be briefly illustrated. One might
say that we know the basic facts about the inter-war years in
Europe; we know what happened, when and to a large extent
why it happened. Debates have taken place around this consensus – about Munich, appeasement, etc. – but these respect the
facts and seek to re-address them only marginally. Often these
debates are linked to specific historians (D. C. Watt, A. J. P.
Taylor) and this is called the historiographical dimension. That is,
historians re-interpret odd bits of the inter-war years and this is
historiographical in that students can study what historians say.

Now certain things follow from this position, not least that if
historiography only takes place on the margins of knowledge,
then an approach that sees all history as historiography (my
view) is also marginalised (i.e. deemed incorrect). Students, I
have often heard it said, should stop looking at what historians
say and concentrate on what actually happened; they should do
some 'proper' history. But this runs counter to all I have been
saying. If history is interpretation, if history is historians'
work(s), then historiography is what the 'proper' study of history
is actually about. In my argument everything is a discursive
construct, including the Skidelsky-like non-interpreted centre;
that is, the so-called centre is just a congealed interpretation.
Here then lies a major difference between Skidelsky and others
and myself. I would like to put forward the following argument to
support my point of view.

Using the inter-war period again, my position is as follows.
Skidelsky among others would argue that a large body of agreed
factual knowledge about 1918–39 exists. Around the edges bits
are re-worked, but the main body stands. And it is not unusual
for these authors to characterise these marginal debates to be
between 'left' and 'right'. This model can be shown thus:

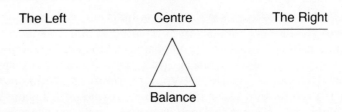

The Left	Centre	The Right

Balance

Here the balanced centre looks undisputed. And it suggests that a 'balanced' historian occupying this centre can look objectively at the points for and against the opposing views of left and right and weigh them up. One can be 'liberal' (non-ideological) in this centre because the ideological positions are out there, on the left and right, and if one or the other wins then this will cause an imbalance. One can adjudicate disinterestedly from this centre: 'on the one hand – on the other'.

But reconsider. Let me now put the left, centre and right on a continuous spectrum. Thus the old model,

The Left	Centre	The Right

Balance

becomes

The Left	Centre	The Right

Spectrum   Spectrum

Balance

Here we immediately see that the centre is not really a centre of anything. Rather, what we have is an ensemble of left/centre/right positions towards one end of a given (and logically infinite) spectrum. Hence, when one allegedly answers in a balanced way from the 'centre', one wants to know the centre of what? For shift the left/centre/right ensemble anywhere on the spectrum and see how the centre is not so much de-centred as the whole concept becomes problematic: a spectrum cannot have a centre.

If this still appears a little vague let me tighten the rachet a further notch. One might ask whether, in England today, marginal/oppositional interpretations, to which we can add and which we can judge, revolve around a Marxist–Leninist centre?

I think the answer is no. But why not? After all there are a great many Marxist–Leninist accounts of 1918–39 around (on fascism, the causes of the Great Patriotic War etc.), so why isn't this the (non-interpretative/given) centre around which other accounts are but marginal interpretations? This is not an unrealistic example because in the USSR Marxist–Leninist accounts are in the centre. In the USSR our 'shared' centre is 'bourgeois'; is on their margins. In other words 'our' centre is just 'ours'. Skidelsky's argument, that our centre is effectively everyone's (universal) and that there really is a centre that is not just another position, seems fallacious. Rather I think there are no centres as such, but local patterns of dominance and marginality, which are all historiographically constructed and which must be historiographically read. As for all of us, Skidelsky and the specific discourse he occupies (and which in that sense 'occupies him'; that is, makes him the historian he is) positions him, and if we are right about the ideological nature of positions, positions ideologically too: remember there are no histories that are not for someone. Let us now move on to the question of bias.

ON BIAS

The concept of historical (historians') bias is everywhere: in schools, in the aims/objectives of countless history syllabi, at A level, in universities and in fact in almost any assessment of historical texts. It is overtly signalled or tacitly assumed with regard to the reading of documents, primary and secondary traces and evidence. In effect bias (and its detection) is taken to be something that is very meaningful. But is it? Let me run a five stage argument.[10]

First, bias makes sense only if it is used in opposition to un-biased; i.e. some sort of objectivity, even truth: unbiased = run-ning true, as in the game of bowls (can you not see the problem 'of bias' already?)

Second, in historical work, bias appears most regularly in em-piricist history, that is, history of a specific type. Empiricist his-tory is committed to the idea that somehow the past can be re-created objectively. Typically the historian goes to the original traces, constructs these as evidence, scrupulously footnotes, etc., and on the basis of this gives a fully documented account. Of course empiricists – like Elton – know that definitive accounts are unachievable but they still aim for them. The ambition is to let the facts speak 'for themselves', unmediated by the bulk of the ven-triloquist-like (and possibly biased) historian.

Because this type of approach has objectivity at its centre then within it bias makes sense. Here bias means the skewing of sources to fit an argument, the withholding of documents, the falsification of evidence . . .

But, and this is point three, history can be things other than empiricist (think back here only to Marwick's twenty-five var-ieties). So, for example, history can be seen as the way groups/classes make sense of the past by making it theirs: here the past can be constructed meaningfully for Marxists, right-radicals, feminists, etc. Of course, within each of these constructs there will be checking mechanisms for validating the readings given (references in footnotes to sources, etc.) but within these discourses the word 'bias' hardly appears. Thus within, say, Marxism, one will see references to many different (party) lines: one might read of voluntarist or economistic tendencies, Gram-scian or Althusserian readings, Trotskyist deviations and so on. But these lines will not be referred to as biases because everyone knows that Gramscians will use the past differently to econom-istic Marxists, so what sense does it make to say Gramsci 'was biased' – against what unbiased account? A Trotskyist one, a bourgeois one – the facts?

Point four. Looking at history this way – as a series of readings all of which are positioned – then there is clearly no unpositioned criterion by which one can judge the degree of bias. In fact it arguably makes little sense to use the term generally – to say for instance that feminists are biased – for they merely have to ask if that judgement is made from a patriarchal position. Not only that. The empiricist claim – that one can detect bias and expunge it by attending scrupulously to 'what the sources say' – is undercut by the fact that sources are mute. It is historians who articulate whatever the 'sources say', for do not many historians all going (honestly and scrupulously in their own ways) to the same sources, still come away with different accounts; do not historians all have their own many narratives to tell?

Point five accordingly becomes a question and an answer to it. The question is: but if this is the case, if bias best makes sense (a) within empiricism and (b) if its claims to get to the truth through some source-led account is problematic and (c) if blanket statements of the type 'feminists are just biased' makes little sense, then why is the term 'bias' in general use? I think the answer could be that:

1 Bias is 'central' to the empiricist mode.
2 This mode (getting the facts to speak allegedly for themselves) is connected, not logically or necessarily but historically (contingently) to liberalism. Here one learns to adjudicate, to weigh things up and to see both sides; here one can pursue the past for its own sake (for the love of it) as it apparently speaks unaided. This mode is ensconced in schools, colleges, universities: it is, is it not, the dominant mode in our social formation.
3 Because this mode is dominant it therefore acts as if its way of doing things is the only way: it universalises itself. But in so doing empiricism not only universalises its (relative) successes but its failures too. As we know, empiricism's major problem is the ascertaining of truth in that it recognises its truths to be, ultimately, interpretation. It does not want to face this; so to ward off this reality it holds to the notion of the true account, claiming such truth is attainable if bias is detected and wiped away. But if everything is ultimately interpretation and if one person's bias is another person's truth, what then? Thus, the problem of bias is specifically an empiricist one but because it is the dominant approach then its problems get distributed as if

they were everyone's. But they are not. Of course – and this must be stressed – other discourses have their own problems of internal coherence, etc., but bias is not the way they are expressed.

To conclude. Students in our culture are likely to meet the concept of bias everywhere even though it is problematic only somewhere. Bias, if and when it is used, ought to be used specifically and locally. (As it is, it is used ideologically.) Elsewhere, because what is constructed as history is constructed differently, the problems of veracity are dealt with differently too.

ON EMPATHY

Empathy, like bias, is a term you will surely have met before.[11] Here the basic question is whether empathy – the claim that one has to get into an informed appreciation of the predicaments and viewpoints of people in the past in order to gain real historical understanding (to see the past from its point of view) – is actually possible? If it is not, and that is my view, then why should attempting the impossible be so high on the agenda? I will approach 'empathy' by looking initially at why I think empathizing effectively is impossible; second I will examine the pressures that have put it so high on the agenda; and finally I will offer some concluding thoughts.

I consider empathy is unachievable for four reasons. Two are basically philosophical and two are practical.

The philosophical problem of 'other minds', as discussed by Wittgenstein and others,[12] considers whether it is possible to enter into the mind of another person we know well and who is beside one, and concludes that it is not. Historians, however, have disregarded this conclusion and have continued to raise questions that are based on the assumption that it actually is possible to enter lots and lots of minds, even minds we cannot possibly know well, and which are far away from us in space and time.

This links into the second philosophical problem. For what is effectively ignored in empathy is that in every act of communication there is an act of translation going on; that every act of speech (speech–act) is an 'interpretation between privacies'. And when, as suggested, this act of translation is not between 'you and me' here and now, but 'us and them' somewhere else and at some other time, then the task is extremely problematic. For to all past events historians bring their own mind-set programmed in the present. As Steiner says:

> Croce's dictum 'all history is contemporary history' points directly to the ontological paradox of the past tense. Historians are increasingly aware that the conventions of narrative and of implicit reality with which they work are philosophically vulnerable. The dilemma exists on at least two levels. The first is semantic. The bulk of the historian's material consists of utterances made in and about the past. Given the perpetual process of linguistic change not only in vocabulary and syntax but in meaning, how is he to interpret, to translate his sources. . . . Reading a historical document, collating the modes of narrative in previous written history, interpreting speech–acts performed in the distant or nearer past, he finds himself becoming more and more of the translator in the technical sense. . . . And the meaning thus arrived at must be the 'true one'. By what metamorphic magic is the historian to proceed?[13]

Steiner's point seems to me to be basic, and he goes on to stress the impossibility of getting into other times: 'When we use past tenses . . . when the historian "makes history" (for that is what he is actually doing), we rely on what I shall call . . . *axiomatic fictions*'[14] (that is, contemporary and overwhelmingly dominant assumptions about what in the main constitutes historical knowledge).

Given then that there is no presuppositionless interpretation of the past, and given that interpretations of the past are constructed in the present, the possibility of the historian being able to slough off his present to reach somebody else's past on their terms looks remote. This is a point picked up by Terry Eagleton in *Criticism and Ideology* where he poses the same problem for the literary critic. The job of the literary critic is, it seems, to tell us what the text under study is about; to make it better understood so that it is easier to read. But in helping the reader to read better (just as the historian's putative task is to help us read the past better) how, asks Eagleton, can the interpreter's (historian's) bulk not get in the way? Here is Eagleton on the problem of reading texts – I have added the bracketed words:

> It is difficult to see criticism [history] as anything but an innocent discipline. Its origins seem spontaneous, its existence natural: there is literature [the past] and so – because we wish to understand and appreciate it – there is also criticism [history] . . . . But . . . criticism [history] as a handmaiden to literature [the past] prevents [such understanding] everywhere. . . . If the task of criticism [history] is to smooth the troubled passage between text [the past] and reader, to elaborate the text [past] so that it may be more easily consumed, how is it to avoid interposing its own ungainly bulk between product and consumer, *over*shadowing its object . . . . It seems that criticism [history] is caught here in an insoluble contradiction.[15]

These then are some of the philosophical problems empathy faces: of the 'translation between privacies', of the 'ontological paradox of the past tense'; of the present-minded historian getting 'back to the past' uncluttered by all that has made him/her modern. Further to these problems, empathy has two practical difficulties to overcome.

The first is a reminder of the discussions in chapter 1 regarding history as theory/practice. In theory the historian is working within all kinds of assumptions of an epistemological, methodological and ideological kind, and we have also seen the practical problems of making histories (the long weekends, pressures from work, publishers, literary style . . .), all of which are inscribed (written into) the historian's own mind. How then is this – the very stuff that allows the historian to think historically in the first place – to be got rid of so that he/she can think 'the past' ('pastically')?

The second problem we might consider is one arising if we transfer the points we have made into a class situation/examination. Let us imagine we are facing an empathy question; we are to try and empathise with Thomas Cromwell's intention to reform Tudor government. What did he see as the problems; how did he see the situation?

As students we might read about Cromwell; we might read (again) Elton or other authorities. We might also read documents relevant to the debate. We may disagree wth some interpretations (enter into the debate) but if we are to remain with it we really must stay in this discursive field. Along comes the question; what were Cromwell's intentions? Now, we cannot empathise directly with Cromwell because we have reached him indirectly (via Elton) so actually we are empathising less with Cromwell's mind than Elton's. This is underlined when we are asked to put Cromwell's intentions into the meaning-making context. For if in, say, educational institutions, it is in history classes that much of that context is provided (a context the teacher gets from Elton too) and if this is about all the context you as students know (and if you were listening all the time, accurately translating the teacher's speech acts, and if you can still find your notes to read) then requests to put Cromwell into an early sixteenth-century context are actually requests to put him into the context of your class experience. Here we are empathising with what the teacher has in his/her own mind mediated by classroom contingencies; that is, with Elton many times removed. If this were an examination, then checks made by external examiners on the answers so produced are checks against what is in their minds; and so it goes on.

Thus I do not think empathy, as typically understood, is possible for these philosophical and practical reasons, which we have touched on only lightly here. Through a lot of critical reading historians may gain 'tentative understandings' but that is a different matter, and empathy may be marginal in reaching such knowledge. But the point I would like to make here is a different one. As far as I can see, empathy is on the agenda for reasons other than giving you the opportunity to try and do it. Empathy is with us for reasons which come not out of epistemological/methodological problems as such but from three disparate pressures, one of which comes out of schooling, one of which comes from an academic direction, and one of which is clearly ideological.

Let us begin by looking at the pressure of schooling. This pressure emerged largely through educational notions of relevance and personal involvement that started initially in primary schools and then became extended. Thus, think here of those imaginative leaps we might well have been asked to make so that we could pretend to be a fox, a snowflake, an angry king: such appeals were (and are) to make pupils feel involved and engaged;

to personalise teaching and learning. Then, with the extension of comprehensivisation from primary to secondary schools and with the attendant problems of classroom organisation and discipline, so the general trend has been toward the breakdown of hierarchies (streaming etc.) towards an equal (personal) entitlement to the same (whole) curriculum. Today, this personalisation of pedagogy (teaching–learning) has led to personalised assessment procedures (designer assessment) and in some ways the end of this process is approaching: personal profiling and one's own positive/negotiated record of achievement signifying the end of hierarchical (once and for all) examinations (people at the top, people at the bottom). Accordingly, in this democratising context where all pupils bring their equally valid/valued opinions to school, then opportunities for their expression must be encouraged: what do they think of the past, what is history for them, what is their explanation – let them try and put themselves into the mind-set of (their) medieval prince. This is a bespoke syllabus, made to measure, cut to fit. In everyday practice this is the world of individual tasks, of separate worksheets, of the personal topic, of the private study, of the project, of the dissertation . . . such approaches here spill over into the academic.

The second pressure is the academic. In England this pressure relies heavily on the specific way of looking at history (idealism) which is associated with the historian R. G. Collingwood. In a nutshell, Collingwood argued that all history is the history of mind, an apparently difficult concept to grasp (and use) when retained within Collingwood's own sophisticated discourse, but when summarised easily understood, not least because by now much of the argument will be familiar.

This, briefly, is Collingwood's argument. Humans are language animals. Through language things are given meaning. These symbolic codes (languages) refer to the world but word and world are categorically different. In different social formations, in different cultures, people speak/spoke differently: the past is a foreign country – people spoke differently there. As Steiner puts it:

> Different civilisations, different epochs do not necessarily produce the same 'speech mass'; certain cultures speak less than others; some modes of sensibility prize taciturnity and

elision, others reward prolixity and semantic orna-
mentation.[16]

So, for instance, the actual/potential vocabulary of medieval
peasant or viking was minuscule compared to ours today. To
understand the medieval peasant/viking is thus to understand
their discourses through the examination of the surviving traces
of them: field patterns, monastic records, chronicles, etc.; these
are manifestations of their intentions and concerns, embodi-
ments of these people's needs; who wanted them for certain
things. In effect understanding history for Collingwood is therefore understanding why these people wanted these things and
nothing else: in a phrase, all history is about the history of what
they had in mind; all history is thus the history of mind(s).
Consequently, to gain historical knowledge we must get inside
such cultural remains/traces to the minds that infused them with
life, to see the world as they did. Accordingly it is this idealist
pressure, variously construed, that legitimates the empathetic
approach for many historians, and indeed for some this academic
argument is what empathy really is. But I think there is more to it
than that. For empathy as constructed by schooling and idealism
needs ideology to complete it. And crucially so. Because it is in
ideology that the major characteristics of empathy are found.
This ideology is liberal, and not any kind of liberalism either, but
one harking back to, and thus being best explained by, a brief
résumé of J. S. Mill's idea of reciprocal freedom.

Central to Mill's idea of freedom was the notion that the individual could do what he/she desired so long as the exercise of that
desire did not curtail the liberty of others. To calculate if this
would occur as a consequence of any action, the person (agent)
had to imagine what these consequences would be; to put him-
self/herself into other people's positions; to see their point of
view. In doing so this calculation would have to be both rational
and universalisable, capable of rational reciprocation for all involved. For if the person(s) affected were ever in a position to do
the same thing back to the agent then mutual harm could occur.
This therefore suggested a pragmatic weighing up and a balancing of viewpoints, a consideration of the pros and cons (on the
one hand – on the other) and the banishment of all extremes as
rational choices for action.

This approach – being rational, seeing other people's views and balancing the options and thus the possibly hurtful consequences of extreme actions (extremism) – is thus what lies behind all those requests to put oneself into another person's position (in the past); to try to see things from their perspective, to rationally calculate their options and to be 'open minded'. This is why, of course, so many empathy questions are problem-solving exercises.

In the middle of this activity, then, is rationality and balance. Here, empathy draws all reasonable people into the centre. Here liberal ideology is at work, working to construct us as liberals. Consequently it is doubtful if this produces what this exercise is ostensibly about – understanding history. Rather the reverse, for what this approach does is to universalise throughout space and time a very local and time-bound ideology, liberalism, to the calculation of interests *per se*, thus putting into the minds of all people (including medieval peasants and vikings who did not know of liberalism and who had unfortunately never had the pleasure of reading J. S. Mill) Mill's own mind.

This is ironic. The only way to bring people in the past (who were so different to us) under our control is to make them the same as us, propelled everywhere by rational calculation, liberal style. Here at the heart of the argument that this is the way of gaining historical understanding we find the very essence of what it means to think a-historically; quite literally anachronistically.

So schooling, idealism and ideology thus constitute empathy, and these are three pressures that do not sit easily together. The pedagogy of personal involvement puts a stress on the imagination that most historians see as suspiciously 'fictional', whilst the problem between idealism – with its stress on the strangeness of the past – and liberal ideology, which stresses the constancy of human beings/human nature *homo economicus* style, are really quite different views as to how (and why) 'knowledge' of the past is possible. And in fact this last point helps explain why, at the moment of writing, empathy is one of the most discussed aspects of 'what history is', an ideological discussion that needs to be understood in order to see both what is going on and why so much seems to be at stake politically in these matters.

As we have seen, the attempt to get into the otherness of the past is, for idealists, what is at the centre of historical study. But this requires some imagining, no matter how much one is enriched by understandings of that past, and it is this stress on imagination that has been attacked. This attack has come mainly from liberal and right-wing empiricists. For they think (if I may generalise) that empathy is basically a waste of time. As empiricists they want to get to 'the facts' and thus 'know' the past that way, but they also know that most of the facts are missing so that knowledge ultimately eludes them. So, to make their accounts as full as possible, they have to do their own bit of imagining (interpreting) to fill the gaps. Here the problem is that if people in the past thought all kinds of odd things, then how can historians imagine accurately? The answer has been to deny that oddness of people in the past, and to stress the 'constancy of human nature' argument which says that, stripped of their culture, all people are and always have been basically the same. That way you can then fill in the gaps accurately because you work on the assumption that faced with the same situation all people would act predictably by (somehow) throwing off their cultural straitjackets and acting naturally. Consequently you don't need empathy – you don't need idealism – because these ideas encourage you to imagine that people in the past are always culture-bound, are never natural, and therefore that you can never really know what they had in mind.

From the liberal–right empiricist position this is the problem, for two reasons. First, it can lead to relativistic scepticism. Second, it may lead to the possibility of people today imagining that other (universalisable) responses were made by people in the past – say, socialist ones. In fact much of the empathy debate has been tied up with these critiques of 'left interpretation'; about whether these imaginative spaces that will always exist will be filled by the correct 'human nature' or not. My own thoughts on this and on empathy in general are as follows.

I think people in the past were very different to us in the meanings they gave to their world, and that any reading on to them of a constancy of human nature type, of whatever kind, is without foundation. I mean, which sort of human nature do you want to pick? I don't think this need lead to scepticism about knowing 'history' because, to repeat, when we study history we are not studying the past but what historians have constructed about the past. In that sense, whether or not people in the past had the same or different natures to us is not only undecidable but also not at issue. In that sense, the past doesn't enter into it. Our real need is to establish the presuppositions that historians take to the past. It would therefore be more constructive (though again ultimately impossible) to try and get into the minds of historians rather than the minds of the people who lived in the past and who only emerge, strictly speaking, through the minds of historians anyway, a task this whole book is encouraging. Not so much 'all history as the history of past people's minds' then, but 'all history as the history of historian's minds'.

ON PRIMARY AND SECONDARY SOURCES; ON SOURCES AND EVIDENCE

Much ink has been spilt over the issue of primary and secondary sources. Clearly there is a difference between primary sources (traces of the past) and secondary texts. As you will know, this difference breaks down especially at the secondary level where it is obviously possible to use a secondary text as a primary source. Thus, for instance, E. P. Thompson's *Making of the English Working Class* can be read both as an introduction to aspects of the industrial revolution and as a study of what a certain kind of Marxist historian like Thompson had to say about it in the late 1950s and early 1960s: same text, different use. But if this is obvious, then why this section on primary and secondary sources: what is the problem?

It is this. I have argued we can never really know the past; that there are no centres; that there are no 'deeper' sources (no sub-text) to draw upon to get things right: all is on the surface. As we saw in chapter 1, in doing research historians do not go down but across, moving laterally in the construction of their accounts from one set of sources to another, effectively doing comparative work. If this is not seen; if you use the word 'source' instead of 'trace'; if you refer to some of these sources as primary and if you sometimes replace primary by original (original and thus under-lying/fundamental source), this suggests that if you go to the originals, then because originals seem genuine (as opposed to secondary/second-hand traces), genuine (true/deep) knowledge can be gained. This prioritises the original source, fetishises documents, and distorts the whole working process of making history. At root is that perpetual quest for truth, the quest also apparent in desires for empathetic understanding – to get back into the genuine minds of the original people so that their views are unadulterated by ours.

If we do not have these ideas, if we are freed from the desire for certainty, if we are released from the idea that history rests on the study of primary/documentary sources (and that doing history is studying these alone and that from these originals we can adjudicate later historians' disagreements), then we are free to see history as an amalgam of those epistemological, methodological, ideological and practical concerns I have outlined.

Having made these points, the debate over evidence need not detain us long. Indeed, were it not for the fact that the 'problem of evidence' is part of the Carr–Elton dispute that is still running and still causing problems in introductory courses on the nature of history, then it really need not detain us at all at this stage.

The point at issue, however, is this. Does the evidence of the past press itself so irresistibly upon the historian that he/she can do no other than allow it to speak for itself, as Elton has suggested, or does evidence, construed now as an absolutely mute resource, need to be quite literally articulated by the historian who, in putting his or her own voice over the evidence *per se*, effectively silences it. At stake here, yet again, is the question of the type and degree of freedom that the past allows the historian to act as interpreter, expressed, this time, as the 'evidence question'.

This problem can be considered in two ways, the first by seeing that the Carr–Elton rendition of the problem rests on an elementary linguistic confusion, the second by re-articulating, rather differently and suggestively, the past–history distinction.

The reason why this specific debate over evidence rests on a terminological confusion is that the term evidence is being applied, especially by Elton, to the same materials when these materials appear in different contexts and therefore need to be understood and called different things. Elton uses the term evidence to describe the sources that the historian goes to when carrying out research ('the evidence is in the record') whereas he ought to have referred to them as, say, traces of the past. By calling such traces evidence, however, Elton gives the impression

– which of course he wants to give – that such pristine pieces of evidence always already organise themselves into latent explanations, so that when enough of them have been found and collected together, then such 'evidence-based' explanations can simply become manifest by themselves, irrespective of the predilection of the humble historian who, professionally, then 'bows down before their weight' (extraordinary metaphors these but understandable in terms of the notion of the sovereignty of the past which one has a duty to serve, etc.). Carr, on the other hand, much more 'bolshy', realises that it is the active historian who does all the work of organising the past's traces (and who thus deserves all the credit), and that the kinds of explanations the traces can be found to support depend upon the type of organisation being practised. In Carr's argument, therefore, the trace only becomes evidence when it is used to support an argument (interpretation) prior to which, although it exists, it remains just an unused piece of stuff from the past. This seems perfectly acceptable to me and clarifies the position muddied by Elton's terminology. However, one of the reasons why the Carr position hasn't been seen to be conclusive within the parameters of 'the debate' (and thus partly why the debate has been perpetuated) is not least because Carr himself sometimes used the word 'evidence' in places where he should have retained the term 'source' (trace), thus finding himself in the paradoxical position of apparently arguing that the evidence is both there before it is used but that it only really becomes evidence when it has been used. The way out of this Carr–Elton debate is therefore to be consistent and not use the term 'evidence' ambiguously. By which I mean we simply remember the salient points: (a) the past occurred; (b) traces of it remain; (c) these traces are there whether the historian goes to them and finds them or not; (d) evidence is the term used when (some or other) of these traces are used 'in evidence' on behalf of (some or other) argument (interpretation) and not before. Evidence, therefore, as opposed to traces, is always the product of the historian's discourse simply because, prior to that discourse being articulated, evidence (history) doesn't exist: only traces do (only the past did).

At this point we can move to the second way of resolving the evidence problem; or rather we can, by recasting the points made in the last paragraph and by again working the past–history distinction, underline the Carr-like argument that the past's hold on history is really the historian's hold on history; that the past, itself, in some sort of pre-discursive way, quite literally 'doesn't have a say in it'.

The argument here – one that when developed pushes the Carr–Elton debate on to more rigorous grounds – is that contrary to what Elton is effectively claiming, the evidence of the past *per se* cannot act logically as a check on the historian's free play because, constituted by discourse, as an effect of discourse, it cannot be made to function as a cause of discourse or as a pre-discursive check (on itself). This (perhaps difficult) point has been explained by Roland Barthes in *The Discourse of History* where he attacks those historians – in our context Elton – who want to deliver 'true' accounts as guaranteed by the 'raw evidence' of the 'real' (the real past). Barthes argues that such historians perform a sleight of hand whereby the referent (the 'thing' the historian refers to) is projected into a realm supposedly beyond discourse from which position it can then be thought of as preceding and determining the discourse which in fact posited it as referent in the first place. According to Barthes this paradox governs the distinctiveness of historical discourse: 'the fact [the evidence] can only have a linguistic existence, as a term in a discourse, and yet it is exactly as if this existence were merely the "copy" . . . of another existence situated in the . . . domain of the "real". This type of discourse is . . . [one] in which the referent is aimed for as something external to the discourse without it ever being possible to attain it outside this discourse.'[17] We can leave it there.

ON COUPLETS: ON CAUSATION, ETC.

The couplets to be referred to here are cause and effect, continuity and change, and similarity and difference. What I intend to do is problematicise them, not in the sense that they are generally taken unproblematically as 'heartland' concepts – an argument I have already rebutted – but to question further the common assumption that these concepts actually can be used unproblem-atically; that is, that it is almost routinely easy to ascertain, say, the causes and consequences of an event. In fact this is not the case. Although these couplets are said to be the ones historians use all the time, it is extremely doubtful if they succeed in using them very rigorously. Accordingly I will examine just one of the concepts, causality, and raise some questions about it that might then be applied to the others.

Let me start to raise these questions by way of posing some. When you are told that history is partly about the way that historians find the causes of past events, with which theories of causal explanation are you presented? Marxist, structuralist, phenomenological, hermeneutic? Anything? When you combine causal factors in terms of the various weight they may have exerted on some event, when the question of their relative influence *vis-à-vis* each other is raised, how do you do the discriminating? If you were asked now to explain the causes of the French Revolution of 1789, what would you do?

Consider this question then: 'how far back and how far afield would it be necessary to go to give a satisfactory analysis of the necessary and sufficient causes of 1789?'

How do you answer this? Does Marxism tell you? Does structural-functionalism? Does an Annales approach?

If one of these does; if, say, Marxism lays down a method of proceeding (crudely, economic conditions must be considered as basic determinants of superstructural changes within the thesis of class struggle; crudely, by involving methodological abstractions, etc.), then how do you work this in detail? For example, how far back do you (have to?) take the influence of economics (to 1783, 1760, 1714, 1648?) and what, exactly, do you include in this category of the economic? How, within the economic, do you know when aspects of it play a decisive role and then lie relatively dormant, determining 'in the last instance'? Again, how far afield will you go: is France metaphorically an island or inextricably caught up within a general European trajectory? What counts as Europe in the eighteenth century? Does America? Again, how do you measure the various levels and degrees of interpenetration between, say, the economic, the political, the social, the cultural, the ideological; and what goes into these categories? Again, how far would your analysis depend upon everyday contingencies: the types of material available, the times of access to it; on the time you have been given and give yourself to answer the question, etc.? Again, what sort of philosophical minefields and stipulated definitions lurk in the terms satisfactory, necesssary, sufficient and analysis? And so on . . . I mean, how do you begin to tackle all the causal factors and complexity of analysis suggested by just these few obvious questions? Where do such questions end?

At this point you may say well, actually, we do not have questions set like that one. They are more straightforward, thus 'Why did the French Revolution occur in 1789?' Although this may be how questions on 1789 typically read, behind them lies the sorts of questions I have raised; namely, the question of 'Why 1789?' means 'What are the causes of 1789?' such causes apparently being an infinite chain spreading backwards and outwards which you somehow have to cut into despite the fact that no method (and no amount of experience) can provide you with any logical or definitive cut in (or 'cut out') points in order to give a sufficient and necessary explanation.

The problem will not go away; so how do you do it? I think that the answer that actually operates in the main is that you copy other people. That is, you know you have something like a satisfactory answer to the question of 1789 because your answer looks and reads like other people's operating in the same discourse – give or take the odd lapse or innovation. Learning history is very much about learning how to play the game in the same way as those already in the game (in the trade) do. In that sense learning history is like practising a craft, like serving an apprenticeship, so that you know you have a satisfactory analysis because it has been constructed from, say, published secondary texts (books, articles, essays) by master-craftsmen who are also trying to explain 1789 – texts by Hobsbawm, Hampson, Schama. Doing history in the main is therefore not all that rigorous theoretically with regard to even some of its most central preoccupations such as trying to explain why things happened, and few A level or undergraduate courses consider systematically and in depth the methodological problems lying in ambush for those who would actually like to know what they are doing. Naturally, all courses could do and they all ought to, and throughout I have footnoted various texts which explore method. Having said that, we can remind ourselves that we should not be surprised at this lacuna in 'training'. For as I mentioned in chapter 1, the dominant discourse is not too interested in the explicit probe for methodological clarity, for that can be picked up (for goodness' sake!) by practising 'proper history' (that is, so the mythology goes, that in the practice of seeking to explain what happened in the past by providing a precise reconstruction of events reported in primary sources and contextualised in certain secondary ones, and by suppressing as much as possible the impulse to interpret or by indicating in the narrative when the facts are merely being represented and when they are being interpreted, so one naturally learns what to do).[18] No, what the dominant discourse is interested in (though here again not always consciously) is arguably the transmission of a certain type of historical culture (which it considers as *the* historical culture) so that what is crucial is that, within the academic articulation of that preference, you begin to copy such academics effectively. At these levels of history you are being inducted into a specific type of academic discourse where it is your ability to internalise it and then write it down (to pass on; to pass the 'tests') that is crucial. Here is Terry Eagleton writing about what the academic study of literature is predominantly about (for 'literature' read 'history'):

> Becoming certified by the state in literary studies [A level, degrees, etc.] is a matter of being able to talk and write in certain ways. It is this which is being taught, examined and certificated . . . . Nobody is especially concerned about what you say . . . provided [it is] compatible with, and can be articulated within, a specific form of discourse . . . . Those employed to teach you this form of discourse will remember whether or not you were able to speak it long after they have forgotten what you said.
>
> Literary theorists, critics and teachers, then, are . . . custodians of discourse. Their task is to preserve this discourse, extend it and elaborate it as necessary . . . initiate newcomers into it and determine whether or not they have successfully mastered it.[19]

HISTORY: A SCIENCE OR AN ART?

The debate over whether history is a science or an art, still a vibrant topic in 'the nature of history' debates, is a product of nineteenth-century ideology.[20] In the nineteenth century the view was widely held that science was the route to truth, and this idea went across the board from Ranke to Comte to Marx. But none pressed the case so hard for history's scientificity as Marx. Accordingly, from the moment when Marxist socialism started to refer to itself (and be referred to) as 'scientific socialism', so bourgeois theorists were concerned to undercut the sciences as such in order to catch in their nets the scientific/certaintist pretensions of the left, and they have done so with some success, but only at the expense of undercutting any scientific foundations they might want or need themselves.

Consequently, and drawing heavily on the romantic artists' antipathy towards science, history was to be considered increasingly as 'an art'.[21] Yet, when pressed to go the whole hog and express itself as just another narrative discourse admitting to organising the past through various rhetorical devices, tropes, emplotments and so forth, historians resisted, falling back on the view that history was, after all, a semi-science, in that historian's data did not lend itself to free artistic licence, and that the form and content of their narratives was not a matter of choice but required 'by the nature of the historical materials themselves'. In this way science, noisily kicked out of the front door, was half-heartedly re-admitted through the back, the result being that the oscillation between 'science and art' has remained as part of the internal problematic of mainstream history.

In this regard history is somewhat isolated, in that theorists in neighbouring discourses do not concur with the 'conventional' historians' assumption that art and science are very different ways of reading the world, having long seen through the ideological locus of the dichotomy that historians have in general mis-recognised and which they have thus retained as being really a problem of epistemology and method. The reason for this continuation of the debate is therefore due not least to that antipathy towards theory which I noted in the Introduction as a characteristic afflicting historians, an affliction underlined by the observation of Hayden White that, since the middle of the nineteenth century, most historians have affected a kind of wilful methodological naïveté:

> as history has become increasingly professionalised and specialised, the ordinary historian, wrapped up in the search for the elusive document that will establish him as an

authority in a narrowly defined field, has had little time to inform himself of the latest developments in the more remote fields of art and science. Many historians are not aware, therefore, that the radical disjunction between art and science which their self-arrogated roles as mediators between them presupposes may perhaps be no longer justified.[22]

In effect then, in the epistemological and methodological terms in which the 'art–science' debate is conducted, that debate is *passé*. It can be read, however, as retaining its present vitality through ideological pressures still expressed as 'method' not least because of historians' relatively cavalier attitude towards theory and introspection.

CONCLUSION

Looking back over this chapter it seems that the questions I have been considering as constituting some of the main areas of introductory debate with regard to the nature of history, have clustered around the ramifications of the problematic of truth. I think this is so because practically all the debates generated by and around the 'history question' do in fact have their locus there. Debates over whether the historian's knowledge can be gained objectively and through the 'proper practices', or whether it is intersubjective and interpretive; debates over whether history is value-free or always positioned 'for someone'; debates over whether history is innocent or ideological, unbiased or biased, fact or fancy. Or, again, debates about whether empathy can provide us with real understandings of people who lived in the past; debates about whether we can, by going to the original sources (traces) know genuinely and in depth; debates as to whether those conceptual couplets represent the essence of history, and finally debates as to whether the real secrets of the past will be revealed through the rigours of scientific method or the flair of the artist.

My answers to these questions have been on the side of scepticism. Of course, this follows from my treatment of what I think history is as outlined in chapter 1. There, having made the point that the past and history are in different categories (and thus

constitute an ontological gap) I indicated some of the epistemological, methodological, ideological and practical reasons that
make the transformation of the past into history problematic.
Thus in coming to a series of conclusions that very much queried
the extent to which the past can be known, then, to be consistent,
I was bound to come down against any kind of certaintist knowledge. Thus, *vis-à-vis* the debates, I have had to argue that the
truth(s) of the past elude us; that history is intersubjective and
ideologically positioned; that objectivity and being unbiased are
chimeras; that empathy is flawed; that 'originals' do not entail
anything 'genuine'; that history is, in opposition to it being an art
or a science, something else – something *sui generis*, a worldly,
wordy language game played for real, and where the metaphors
of history as science or history as art, reflect the distribution of
power that put these metaphors into play.

It may be, of course, that this kind of scepticism towards
historical knowledge may lead towards cynicism and varieties of
negativity. But it need not and it does not for me. Along with and
for the same sort of reasons as Hayden White, I see moral relativism and epistemological scepticism as the basis for social toler-
ation and the positive recognition of differences.[23] As White has
put it:

> We do expect that Constable and Cézanne will have looked
> for the same thing in a given landscape, and when we
> confront their respective representations of a landscape, we
> do not expect to have to choose between them and deter-
> mine which is the 'more correct' one . . . when we view the
> work of an artist or . . . a scientist [or historian] we do not ask
> if he sees what we would see in the same general field, but
> whether or not he has introduced into his representation of
> it anything that could be considered false information *for
> anyone who is capable of understanding the system of notation
> used*.
>
>   If applied to historical writing, the methodological and
> stylistic cosmopolitanism which this conception . . . pro-
> motes would force historians to abandon the attempt to
> portray 'one particular portion of life *right side up* and in *true*
> perspective' . . . and to recognise that there is no such thing
> as a *single* correct view. . . . This would allow us to entertain

seriously those creative distortions offered by minds capable of looking at the past with the same seriousness as ourselves but with different ... orientations. Then we should no longer naïvely expect that statements about a given epoch or complex of events in the past 'correspond' to some pre-existent body of 'raw facts'. For we should recognise that *what constitutes the facts themselves* is the problem that the historian ... has tried to solve in the choice of the metaphor by which he orders his world, past, present and future.[24]

It is this kind of approach that I have been concerned to argue for here; a positive reflexive scepticism. This is an attitude that considers knowledge to be a good thing, and that knowledge does not become bad when the sceptical knowledge we now have as a culture, shows us the limits of the certaintist knowledge we once, as a culture, thought we had. Again, by linking history to the powers that constitute it, history may lose its innocence; but if that innocence (of history 'for its own sake') has been the way the dominant discourse has articulated its interests, then in a democratic society this is something we ought to know. In any case, the aim here has been to help you to be reflexive; to develop a self-conscious reflexivity not only of the questions one asks and the answers one accepts, but why one asks and answers in the way one does and not other; further, of what such processes signify in terms of one's position. Such reflexivity ponders over how the discourse one is studying – history – has been written by forces and pressures way beyond its ostensible object of enquiry – the past – forces and pressures that I think can best be understood today by the practices and ideas of post-modernism.

Chapter 3

Doing history in the post-modern world

At various times throughout this text, and not least in the closing words of the last chapter, I have asserted and/or taken it as read that we live in a post-modern world and that this condition affects the sorts of views you and I might hold about history. What I want to do now is to substantiate this assertion and to say a little more about what such views may entail. To do this I have divided this chapter into three sections. First I want to work an already existing definition of post-modernism and look briefly at how the condition it refers to seems to have come into existence. Secondly I will show how this type of post-modernism has produced a situation where there has now developed a mass of historical genres and what some of the implications of this are for history's nature and for historical work. Thirdly I will sketch in an argument about what history perhaps ought to be that does not seek to deny post-modernist consequences but which rather suggests a way of running positively with them; a way of doing history in the post-modern world that again throws light on 'the history question'.

Post-modernism is a difficult area. Because post-modernists see nothing as fixed or solid this jeopardises the sorts of attempts that they may make to define what they see themselves as part of, whilst some commentators have doubted (self-described post-modernists notwithstanding) the very existence of the condition.[1] I have found increasingly that the definition offered by the French philosopher Jean-François Lyotard in *The Post-Modern Condition* is one that I can make sense of and use.[2] It is inevitable that Lyotard should have his detractors and my use of his ideas here does not mean I have simply ignored various critiques. Nevertheless, Lyotard's analysis about that part of the world in which I live – a social formation where under the impact of secularising, democratising, computerising and consumerising pressures the maps and statuses of knowledge are being re-drawn and re-described – is one that I seem to recognise. Lyotard's definition offers a vantage point and a range of concepts from and through which it appears possible to see what is currently going on both in general terms and in just one of the areas being affected, namely history.

Lyotard's definition at its most basic is rather minimal, characterising post-modernism as witnessing the 'death of centres' and of displaying 'incredulity towards metanarratives'. What do these things mean and how can they be explained?

They mean, first of all, that all those old organising frameworks that presupposed the privileging of various centres (things that are, for example, Anglo-centric, Euro-centric, ethno-centric, gender-centric, logo-centric) are no longer regarded as legitimate and natural frameworks (legitimate because natural), but as temporary fictions which were useful for the articulation not of universal but of actually very particular interests; whilst 'incredulity towards metanarratives' means that those great structuring (metaphysical) stories which have given meaning(s) to western developments have been drained of vitality. After the nineteenth-century announcements of the death of God (the theological metanarrative), the death of secular surrogates has occurred. The late nineteenth and the twentieth centuries have seen an undercutting of reason and science which has made problematic all these certaintist discourses built upon them: that whole Enlightenment project; those various programmes of human progress, reform and emancipation that manifested themselves in, say, humanism, liberalism, Marxism, and so on.

Why have such endings occurred? Why this now 'common sense' (of) incredulity? Let me, whilst being conscious of the constructed nature of all historical narratives, offer a brief explanatory story.[3]

Long ago, pre-modern social hierarchies were based overwhelmingly on what were taken to be intrinsic values: divinity, race, blood, lineage. Here what determined a man's position was what he was by birth, by what he had in him, so that a man just

was 'born to rule', a man just was 'born to serve', a man just did
know and have 'his place'. But it was precisely these natural
orders, once the legitimisation of kings, aristocracies and priests,
that were undercut by the commercial, financial and industrial
bourgeoisie. Busy manufacturing all kinds of things, the bourgeoisie began to manufacture itself, coming to express its ambitions through the idea of liberal utility. According to this
theory, men were now to be seen to have value not by virtue of
birth but by effort; what value a person was to have in life was to
be earned not given. Hence the hardworking bourgeoisie soon
located its own value in those external objects that expressed and
embodied its toil – private property. From this position the bourgeoisie was then able to run two critiques that tried to establish its
differences from and importance over everyone else; that is, from
those people whose wealth and property were considered un-
earned (the idle rich) and those who had little or no property to
speak of (the relatively idle poor).

However, this late eighteenth- and early nineteenth-century
legitimation was not to last. In developing the capitalist mode of
production the bourgeoisie developed other things too: a romantic, aristocratic reaction that arguably soured into an élitist *ennui*
to resurface in unpleasant ways in aspects of the twentieth century.[4] Wage labourers, workers who certainly recognised that
they were poor alright but not that they were idle, preferred to be
seen exactly as they were coming to be described, as the *working*
classes. Consequently it was not long before such workers began
to press the same concept of utility that the bourgeoisie had used
against the old regime, against a bourgeoisie which was, from the
workers' perspective, itself relatively unproductive. In this way
the idea of utility provided a sort of 'rough guide to exploitation',
and to it Marx in particular constructed for the working classes
(the proletariat) a much more elaborate philosophical and historical understanding of their position. This was to produce an
ideology which did not value the gaining of some sort of property
by the proletariat so that through it they could then enjoy the
same formal rights and freedoms as the bourgeoisie (the enticing
bourgeois carrot of respectability); but rather the argument was
that the route to substantive freedom was to be via the abolition of
property. Given that the proletariat effectively had no property,
then what better could they value than the one they did own –

themselves. Man, it was argued, had value just by being alive. If living a life was to all intents and purposes prevented by the type of property distribution that existed as capitalism, then such property could go. In the (not so distant) future lay the prospect of a world held in authentic human freedom and in common – communism.

In the USSR in 1917 the communist experiment began. From the start its global ambitions ('workers of the world unite') received set-backs. The universalism of Marxism became localised quickly into national expressions, and its emancipatory end soon became embroiled within the contingencies of dictatorial means. In this way actually existing socialism unintentionally helped to deconstruct its own potential, turning increasingly pessimistic what was once the workers' supremely optimistic metanarrative, Marxism.

Meanwhile, back in the west, two European-based world wars, economic crises, Fascism, Nazism, and the guilt-ridden traumas of de-colonisation, along with further critiques of capitalism by 'western Marxists' (among others Gramsci, the Frankfurt School, Althusser) and more recently, feminists, had finally broken down the last remaining theories underpinning notions of liberal progress, of harmony through competition, of an optimistic belief in the reasonableness of (bourgeois) rational man. In this situation capitalism thus had to find itself another basis for value, and this time it located it in an overt celebration of what had actually always underpinned it but which it had long considered as too risky to expose without some kind of protective human (organicist, humanist, welfarist) face, market forces as such, a theoretical visibility (in monetarism, etc.) that went hand in hand with the extraordinary economic productivity of the post-1950 era.

But, of course, as suspected, such an explicit valorisation of the 'cash-nexus', such a heavy prioritisation of consumer choice, could only be bought at the expense of foregrounding relativism and pragmatism. In the open market commodities have no pretence of possessing intrinsic value; the value of 'goods' lies in what they can be exchanged for, in their exchange-value. In such a market, people too take on the garb of objects, finding their value in external relationships. Similarly, private and public moralities are affected; ethics become personalised and narcissistic, a relative and free-wheeling affair of taste and style: 'You can be anything you like man!' No moral absolutes transcend the everyday. Such relativism and scepticism affect the status of epistemological and methodological practices too; here there are only positions, perspectives, models, angles, paradigms. The objects of knowledge seem to be constructed arbitrarily, thrown together in the manner of collage, montage and pastiche, so that, as Lyotard has expressed it, 'Modernity seems to be . . . a way of shaping a sequence of moments in such a way that it accepts a high rate of contingency.'[5] Here a flexible pragmatism runs (what is good is what pays off) resulting in a series of calculating practices. Accordingly, in a culture as informed by relativism as this, any remaining version of left-wing emancipation – already vitiated by those actual left regimes – has become confused, not least because of the virtual disappearance of the left's (objective) object of enquiry/commitment, the proletariat. Due to the restructuring of older industrial practices in the face of newer entrepreneurial/service ones, then the proletariat, like the heavy industry it owed its composition to, has effectively been decomposed. In its place there is now a series of differences: a small working-class core, a new(ish) underclass, and the rather unstable groupings of (some) youth, the unemployed, blacks, women, gays, Greens.

To bring this story towards a close: in these arguably postist days – post-liberal, post-western, post-heavy industrial, post-Marxist – the old centres barely hold, and the old metanarratives no longer resonate with actuality and promise, coming to look incredible from late twentieth-century sceptical perspectives. ('Fancy anybody ever believing in that!') Possibly no social formation we know of has so systematically eradicated intrinsic value from its culture so much as liberal market capitalism, not through choice, but through the 'cultural logic of late-capital'.[6] Accordingly, as George Steiner has noted, 'it is this collapse, more or less complete, more or less conscious, of those hierarchial, definitional value gradients (and can there be value without hierarchy?) which is now the major fact of our intellectual and social circumstances.'[7]

Post-modernism is the general expression of those circumstances. Post-modernism is not a united movement. It is not a tendency which essentially belongs to either the left of the centre

or the right (at some point on a spectrum) and nor is it a consequence of post-1968 intellectual/Parisian blues.[8] Rather, as circumstances have demanded, aristocratic, bourgeois and left
ideologues (from Nietzsche to Freud to Saussure to Wittgenstein
to Althusser to Foucault to Derrida) have had to reappraise,
across a range of discourses (philosophy, linguistics, politics, art,
literature, history), the bases for their positions as they have
adjusted to the wider socio-economic, political and cultural slip-
pages underfoot. These reappraisals, although conducted very
differently and for oppositional reasons, have all reached the
same conclusion. As they have searched ever harder for some
foundations for their own positions, what they have all realised is
that no such foundations exist either for themselves or for anybody else – and nor have they ever done so: every idol has had
feet made of clay. As a result scepticism or, more strongly, nihilism, just does now provide the dominant, underlying intellectual
presuppositions of 'our times'.[9]

Of course types and degrees of scepticism have long lived
within the 'Western Tradition' (as was mentioned in chapter 2),
but the difference this time is that what had previously been
glimpsed somewhat intermittently and kept largely on the
margins, not only now lies right across our culture, but is also
variously welcomed. For post-modernists not only refuse to
mourn or wax nostalgic for those now ghostly centres and metanarratives (nor for those who mostly benefited from them) but,
for a range of reasons, celebrate or strategically utilise the widely
acknowledged 'incommensurability of reality to concepts'.[10]

This then is what I take to be our post-modern world. This is the
pressure that has allowed, or forced, the perspective on history
that I have sketched out in chapters 1 and 2. And it is this same
pressure – this overbearing circumstance – which has also produced what I now want to go on to consider; the consequential
existence of that whole mass of history genres which currently
surround us and which have helped relativise and historicise
history at the very same time as history began to be widely
expressed through these 'sceptical' characteristics. This is a post-
modern milieu where the concept of 'ironic re-description', as
construed by Richard Rorty, appropriately describes our times

and its various workings of the (its) past, and can serve to introduce those genres.

In *Contingency, Irony and Solidarity*,[11] Rorty has sketched in a figure that he has called the liberal ironist (actually himself). This person is liberal because s/he thinks that acts of cruelty are the worst things that people can do to each other, but s/he is also sufficiently historicist and nominalist enough ('things' are 'words') to have abandoned the idea that such beliefs refer back to some kind of real foundation beyond the reach of time and chance. For the liberal ironist there is no way of demonstrating to someone who wishes to be cruel that it is wrong to be so. What has thus been seen from the end of the eighteenth century until it now lives generally in our culture, says Rorty, is the view that anything can be made to look good or bad, desirable or undesirable, useful or useless, simply by being re-described (just as in my story what counted as value for the aristocrat, bourgeois and proletarian was re-described). And it is this 're-descriptive turn' that has encompassed, of course, the particular thing that we are interested in in this text, the past/history.

For as we have seen, this is a past that can be infinitely re-described. It can and has supported countless plausible and, *vis-à-vis* their own methodological lights, equally legitimate histories; it has unfailingly given whatever historians (and their impersonators) have wanted and want: various births, origins, legitimating antecedents, explanations and lines of descent (Tory, Whig, Marxist etc.) useful for them as they try to be in control, so that they can make the past their past and so say, along with Nietzsche, 'So I willed it.'

Today more people(s) than ever before are willing things. In the wake of those absent centres and collapsed metanarratives, so the conditions of post-modernism have produced that multiplicity of histories that can be met everywhere throughout our democratic/consumerising culture, a mass of genres (designer/niche histories) to be variously used and/or abused.

Here we can identify, say, historians' histories (professional histories attempting to exercise hegemony over the field, a version expressed in the thesis, the monograph and the text), teachers' histories (necessarily popularisations of professional histories), and then a whole range of other distinctive forms that can only be listed: children's histories, popular-memory histories, proscribed histories, black histories, white histories, women's histories, feminist histories, men's histories, heritage histories, reactionary histories, revolutionary histories, bottom-dog histories, top-dog histories, etc., all these varying constructs being affected by local, regional, national and international perspectives.

This is not all. All of these genres have ragged and interlapping edges, all lean on each other and define themselves by what they are not – inter-textuality. Not only that. All are strafed by epistemological, methodological and ideological assumptions that show no one-to-one relationship but which move across the whole field so that we can look at each of these genres now structurally or phenomenologically and then empirically or existentially; from the perspective now of liberalism or Marxism and then from the radical right, combining and re-combining the available elements so that none of the resultant histories has any necessary permanence; is expressive of no essence. What is clear is therefore the utter contingency of readings and the recognition that interpretations at (say) the 'centre' of our culture are not there because they are true or methodologically correct (brilliant histories can be marginalised if their subject matter is unpalatable) but because they are aligned to the dominant discursive practices: again power/knowledge.

This interpretive flux, when viewed positively, is potentially empowering to even the most marginal in that they can at least make their own histories even if they do not have the power to make them other peoples'. As Peter Widdowson has argued, it is unlikely that history can now be rescued from a historiographically led and methodologically informed deconstructionism, 'and nor should it be'.[12] Querying the notion of the historian's truth, pointing to the variable facticity of facts, insisting that historians write the past from ideological positions, stressing that history is a written discourse as liable to deconstruction as any other, arguing that 'the past' is as notional a concept as 'the real world' to which novelists allude in realist fictions – only ever existing in the present discourses that articulate it – all these things destabilise the past and fracture it, so that, in the cracks opened up, new histories can be made.

On the other hand, however, viewed negatively by those who retain enough power to draw up the boundaries of an ostensibly 'proper' history still stubbornly defined by reference to a putative objectivity, then this freedom to make alternative readings seems subversive; it appears challenging. Accordingly it has generally been the case that the dominant discursive practices attempt to close down (effect a closure) on those readings they wish not to run. At our present conjuncture, two such approaches to closure can be seen. Either the dominant practices attempt to recuperate/incorporate unwelcome histories into the mainstream (as in attempts to 'redomesticate' feminist readings by allowing them a proper and respectable place within history *per se* rather than letting them remain her-story); or, ironically, they capitalise on the phenomenon of post-modern pastlessness, turning it (redescribing it) to their advantage.

If the past can be read as an endless circulation of insubstantial interests and styles, then this applies not only to the more dominant readings but to newer alternative ones too. For while there may be a sense in which everyone is in the same boat, because not all the boat's occupants are in the same position, in that some already have their histories in place, this problematicisation of the foundations for historical building is held to be more damaging for those whose constructions are at an early stage. Widdowson again: 'In this scenario, post modernism is the last great gambit of capitalism to [try and] defeat opposition, contestation and change . . . "We are left in a world of radically 'empty' signifiers. No meaning. No classes. No history. Just a ceaseless procession of simulacra; the past is played and replayed as an amusing range of styles, genres, signifying practices to be combined and re-combined at will. . . . The only history that exists here is the history of the signifier and that is no history at all . . . ."'[13]

My own view on these 'possibilities' that post-modernism has constituted at the very same time as allowing expression, is that such attempts at *status quo* recuperation and closure are unlikely to be effective within the trajectory of democratising, sceptical/ironic social formations and that, *après* Widdowson, they ought not to be anyway. Between the Scylla and Charybdis of, on the one hand, authorised history and, on the other, post-modern pastlessness, a space exists for the desirable outcome of as many people(s) as possible to make their own histories such that they can have real effects (a real say) in the world. To be sure, in their direction and in their impact these effects cannot be guaranteed with precision or (much to the chagrin of, say, Marxist underwriters) definitively underwritten.[14] But they can occur and one can help them. For viewed not in its traditional guise as a subject discipline aiming at a real knowledge of the past, but seen rather as what it is, a discursive practice that enables present-minded people(s) to go to the past, there to delve around and reorganise it appropriately to their needs, then such history, as the cultural critic Tony Bennett has argued, may well have a radical cogency that can make visible aspects of the past that have previously been hidden or secreted away; that have previously been overlooked or sidelined, thereby producing fresh insights that can actually make emancipatory, material differences to and within the present – which is where all history starts from and returns to.

I now come to the third and final section of this chapter. Here I want to suggest a way in which it might be possible to run 'historically' with the consequences of post-modernism as outlined above in the positive direction of democratic emancipation; a democratic emancipation that at one and the same time further clarifies the question of 'the nature of history'.

In *The Discourse of History*, Roland Barthes has argued that the past can be represented in many historians' modes and tropes some of which, however, are less mythological and mystifying than others inasmuch as they deliberately call overt attention to their own processes of production and explicitly indicate the constructed rather than the found nature of their referents. As far as I am concerned the benefits of this are obvious. To work in this way is to adopt a method which deconstructs and historicises all those interpretations that have certaintist pretensions and which fail to call into question the conditions of their own making; which forget to indicate their subservience to unrevealed interests, which mis-recognise their own historical moment, and which mask those epistemological, methodological and ideological pre-suppositions that, as I have tried to suggest throughout this text, everywhere and everytime mediate the past into history.

How might this desirable approach to history then – an approach designed to develop a democratising critical intelligence laced with irony – be realised? Perhaps two things are needed. First would be what might be termed a reflexive methodology. What this means is that (perhaps as students) you are given an explicit analysis of why the history you are getting is the one you are getting and why you are getting it in the way you are and not in any other. This analysis would work the fertile distinction between the past and history out of which emerges the problematics of 'the history question' that I have begun to introduce and look at in this text. And further, there is then a need for detailed historiographical studies to examine how previous and current histories have been constructed both in terms of their method and their content; and here a further text is needed. What I am suggesting is thus a radical historicisation of history ('always historicise') and I take this as the starting point for a reflexive historian, going on to suggest that, for subsequent historical work, you develop a self-consciously held (and acknowledged) position.

Here a comment about a 'choice of position' is necessary.

For in saying that you ought to make an explicit choice of position I do not want to imply that if you do not want to make such a choice then you can do a 'position-less' history. That is, I do not want to suggest that you have some sort of freedom to choose or not; for this is to be unreflectively liberal. In liberal discourse there is always posited, somewhere and somehow, a sort of neutral ground from which it looks precisely as if you can choose or not. This neutral ground is not seen as another position one already occupies, but is considered rather as a disinterested site from which one can sit back and objectively make unbiased choices and judgements. But we have seen that this is not so. There is no such thing as an 'unpositioned centre' (actually a contradiction in terms); no possibility of an unpositioned site. The only choice is between a history that is aware of what it is doing and a history that is not. Here the comments of the literary theorist Robert Young are to the point (for his 'criticism' read 'reading'):

> No criticism is without an implicit – if not explicit – theoretical position. Thus the complaint levelled against so-called 'theoretical criticism' – that it imposes its theories on to the texts [the past] themselves – is in fact most applicable to so-called 'non-theoretical criticism', whose pre-conceptions

about how to read and what to read for, are so fundamental
that they remain 'natural' . . . free of theory.[15]

Thus, all history is theoretical and all theories are positioned
and positioning. In choosing a position of your own I would thus
obviously not want to impose my way of reading the past on you,
but I would ask you to remember that as you choose you always
select a version of the past and a way of appropriating it that has
effects; that aligns you with some readings (readers) and against
others.[16] The point is this: that those who claim to know what
history is, is for them (as for me) to have always already carried
out an act of interpretation.[17]

And finally, the second thing to help realise a sceptical, critically reflexive approach to both the 'history question' and doing
history, is the selection of a content appropriate for this practice.
Of course, there is a sense in which any part of the past would
suffice for this, given its readiness to oblige any interpreter.
Nevertheless, other things being equal, my own preference
would be for a series of histories that helped us to understand the
world that we live in and the forms of history that have both
helped produce it and which it has produced. This is an ordinary
enough claim but it can be critically twisted somewhat by using a
form of words by Foucault: not so much a history to help us
understand the world in which we live then, but rather a series of
'histories of the present'.

The reason for this choice can be put briefly. If the present can
best be understood as post-modern (and if, as Philip Rieff has
remarked, we can actually survive this experiment called modernity[18]) then this suggests to me that the content of a preferred
history should be studies of this phenomenon. That is, that the
analyses of our modern world via the methodologically informed
perspectives of post-modernism not only help us to locate all
those present debates over 'what is history?' (who is history for?),
but also provide us, at a moment in time that hinges between the
old and the new, with what in a sense all these debates want: a
context that will make an informed and workable answer to that
question possible. In the post-modern world, then, arguably the
content and context of history should be a generous series of
methodologically reflexive studies of the makings of the histories
of post-modernity itself.

Notes

Introduction

1 I use the term discourse throughout this book (e.g. 'to be in control of your own discourse'; 'the discourse of history') in the sense that it relates people's thoughts about history to interests and power. Thus, to be in control of your own discourse means that you have power over what you want history to be rather than accepting what others say it is; this consequently empowers you, not them. Similarly, the use of the phrase 'the discourse of history', means that, rather than seeing history as a subject or a discipline (schoolish terms) which suggests that you just learn something that is always already there in some natural or obvious way and to which you innocently, objectively and disinterestedly respond, you actually see history as a 'field of force'; a series of ways of organising the past by and for interested parties which always comes from somewhere and for some purpose and which, in their direction, would like to carry you with them. This field is a 'field of force' because in it these directions are contested (have to be fought for). It is a field that variously includes and excludes, which centres and marginalises views of the past in ways and in degrees that refract the powers of those forwarding them. Using the term 'discourse', then, indicates that we know that history is never itself, is never said or read (articulated, expressed, discoursed) innocently, but that it is always for someone. This text works on the assumption that knowing this might empower the knower, and that this is a good thing. (Note: This way of using the terms is not the same as that discussed by Hayden White in his introduction to *Tropics of Discourse*, London, Johns Hopkins University Press, 1978; see especially White's technical – and brilliant – Introduction.)

2 E. H. Carr, *What Is History?*, London, Penguin, 1963; G. Elton, *The Practice of History*, London, Fontana, 1969; A. Marwick, *The Nature of History*, London, Macmillan, 1970.

3 J. Tosh, *The Pursuit of History*, London, Longman, 1984.

4 For example: R. Rorty, *Philosophy and the Mirror of Nature*, Oxford,

Blackwell, 1980; R. Rorty, *Contingency, Irony and Solidarity*, Cambridge, Cambridge University Press, 1989; T. Eagleton, *Literary Theory*, Oxford, Blackwell, 1983; J. Frow, *Marxism and Literary History*, Cambridge (Mass.), Harvard University Press, 1986; D. Bromwich, *A Choice of Inheritance*, Cambridge (Mass.), Harvard University Press, 1989.

5 P. Geyl, *Debates with Historians*, London, Fontana, 1962; M. Bloch, *The Historian's Craft*, Manchester, Manchester University Press, 1954; R. Collingwood, *The Idea of History*, Oxford, Oxford University Press, 1946; H. White, *The Content of the Form*, London, Johns Hopkins University Press, 1987; M. Foucault, *Power/Knowledge*, New York, Pantheon, 1980.

6 A. Callinicos, *Making History*, New York, Cornell University Press, 1988; M. Oakeshott, *On History*, Oxford, Blackwell, 1983; R. Chartier, *Cultural History*, Oxford, Polity, 1988; S. Horigan, *Nature and Culture in Western Discourses*, London, Routledge, 1989; E. Wolfe, *Europe and the People Without History*, London, University of California Press, 1982; M. Berman, *All That Is Solid Melts into Air*, London, Verso, 1983; I. Hassan, 'The Culture of Post-Modernism', *Theory, Culture and Society*, 2, 3, 1985, 119–32.

7 G. Stedman-Jones, 'The Poverty of Empiricism', in R. Blackburn (ed.), *Ideology in Social Science*, London, Fontana, 1972; R. Samuel, 'Grand Narratives', *History Workshop Journal*, 29, 1990; D. Cannadine, 'British History: Past, Present – and Future?', *Past and Present*, 116, 1987; C. Parker, *The English Historical Tradition Since 1850*, Edinburgh, Donald, 1990.

8 This does not mean to say that one must be unaware of the danger of history's possible subordination to literary imperialism; thus Bennett: 'the conspectus on the past as an infinite text which can only be endlessly retextualised rests on a transference to the past of literature's own object and procedures. It is a literalisation of the past which must be judged as an attempt to extend the sway of literature's own regime of truth into that of history' (T. Bennett, *Outside Literature*, London, Routledge, 1990, p.280). A self-aware raid on literature's procedures as and when required, then, is more to my point.

9 The chapters have been kept short for several reasons, the main one being the introductory and polemical nature of the text which means that I have not gone in for a general coverage to dip into (e.g. Marwick, op.cit.) but have tried to keep this introductory argument brief enough to be read in one or two sittings and thus kept in mind in one go. I also ought to say that I have not tried to make this text anything other than basic and 'teacherly'. I am aware of the way it has simplified complex areas – for example the history of post-modernism – but my aim has been to put the arguments briefly and then indicate in footnotes the more sophisticated and scholarly treatments one might go to. In other words, I have tried to push further reading toward some of the texts I have used behind the scenes of this book, whilst deliberately keeping most of them out of it.

1   What history is

1   J. Sturrock, *Structuralism*, London, Paladin, 1986, p.56.
2   See, for example, the journal *History and Gender*, Blackwell, which started in 1989; V. Seidler, *Rediscovering Masculinity*, London, Routledge, 1989; E. Showalter, *Speaking of Gender*, London, Routledge, 1989.
3   On the relationship between history and fiction see: H. White, *The Content of the Form*, London, Johns Hopkins University Press, 1987; L. Hutcheon, *A Poetics of Post-Modernism*, London, Routledge, 1988; T. Bennett, *Outside Literature*, London, Routledge, 1990; V. Descombes, *Modern French Philosophy*, Cambridge, Cambridge University Press, 1980, especially chapter 4; H. White, *Tropics of Discourse*, London, Johns Hopkins University Press, 1978, especially chapter 5, 'The Fictions of Factual Representation'.
4   D. Lowenthal, *The Past is a Foreign Country*, Cambridge, Cambridge University Press, 1985, especially chapter 5.
5   S. Giles, 'Against Interpretation', *The British Journal of Aesthetics*, 28, 1, 1988. A similar point, made for very different reasons, is put by Michael Oakeshott in *On History*, Oxford, Blackwell, 1983. For Oakeshott a historically understood past is the conclusion of a critical enquiry of a certain type, 'to be found nowhere but in a history book . . . history is . . . an enquiry in which authenticated survivals from the past are dissolved into their component features in order to be used for what they are worth as circumstantial evidence from which to infer a past which has not survived; a past composed of passages of related historical events . . . and assembled as themselves answers to questions about the past formulated by a historian' (p.33).
6   Lowenthal, op.cit., p.216.
7   G. Steiner, *After Babel*, Oxford, Oxford University Press, 1975, p.234.
8   Lowenthal, op.cit., p.218.
9   ibid., p.218.
10 G. Elton, *The Practice of History*, London, Fontana, 1969, pp.70, 112–13.
11 E. P. Thompson, *The Poverty of Theory*, London, Merlin, 1979, p.193.
12 A. Marwick, *The Nature of History*, London, Macmillan, 1970, pp.187, 190.
13 D. Steel, 'New History', *History Resource*, 2, 3, 1989.
14 J. H. Plumb, *The Death of the Past*, London, Macmillan, 1969, *passim*.
15 P. Wright, *On Living in an Old Country*, London, Verso, 1985.
16 A fuller treatment of these sorts of practices can be found in M. Stanford, *The Nature of Historical Knowledge*, Oxford, Blackwell, 1986, especially chapter 4 onwards.
17 R. Scholes, *Textual Power*, London, Yale University Press, 1985; T. Eagleton, *Criticism and Ideology*, London, New Left Books, 1976; S. Fish, *Is There a Text in This Class?*, Cambridge (Mass.), Harvard University Press, 1980; T. Bennett, op.cit.,
18 This definition is not unlike that arrived at for literature by John Frow,

Marxism and Literary History, Cambridge (Mass.), Harvard University Press, 1986. For Frow, literature 'designates a set of practices for signification which have been socially systematised as a unity and which in turn regulate the production, the reception, and the circulation of texts assigned to this category. It thus constitutes a common form of textuality for formally and temporally disparate texts, although this shared space may be riven by antagonistic regimes of signification corresponding to different class (or race or gender or religious) positionings and their different institutional bases' (p.84).

2 On some questions and some answers

1 G. Steiner, *Real Presences*, London, Faber, 1989, p.71.
2 ibid., p.1.
3 Quoted in A. Sheridan, *Foucault: The Will to Truth*, London, Tavistock, 1980, p.46.
4 Steiner, op.cit., pp.93–5.
5 R. Rorty, *Contingency, Irony and Solidarity*, Cambridge, Cambridge University Press, 1989, p.3.
6 M. Foucault, *Power/Knowledge*, New York, Pantheon, 1981, pp. 131–3.
7 G. Steiner, *After Babel*, Oxford, Oxford University Press, 1975, p.110, *passim*.
8 Of course I do not in this text deny the existence of the actuality of the past but only that, logically, that past cannot entail one and only one evaluation of it (re: the fact–value distinction, which of course, very obviously, admits of 'facts'). I do not, moreover, deny that the term 'truth' has a literal meaning in certain discourses as a 'truth effect'. But, as 'truth' is a term that is applied only to statements in analytical contexts (e.g. deductive logic) and not to the wider contexts themselves of which statements are but one kind of linguistic construct, then historians, involved as they are in such wider arguments (interpretations) cannot refer to these wider arguments/ interpretations as true. In fact to speak of a 'true interpretation' is a contradiction in terms. See Oakeshott on this (*On History*, Oxford, Blackwell, 1983, p.49, *passim*) and F. R. Ankersmit, 'Reply to Professor Zagorin', *History and Theory*, 29, 1990, 275–96. See also the background to Ankersmit: F. R. Ankersmit, 'Historiography and Post-modernism', *History and Theory*, 28, 1989, 137–53, and P. Zagorin, 'Historiography and Post-modernism: Reconsiderations', *History and Theory*, 29, 1990, 263–74. See also R. Rorty, *Consequences of Pragmatism*, Minneapolis, University of Minnesota Press, 1982, and H. White, *Tropics of Discourse*, London, Johns Hopkins University Press, 1978.
9 R. Skidelsky, 'A Question of Values', *The Times Educational Supplement*, 27.5.1988. Skidelsky is one of those historians who seem to believe that different interpretations of the same set of events are the result of ideological distortions or inadequate factual data, arguing, in effect, that if one only eschewed ideology and remained true to the facts then certain knowledge would appear. But, as White has

argued, in the unprocessed record of the past and in the chronicle of events which the historian extracts from the record, the facts exist only as a congeries of contiguously related fragments which then need to be put together through some enabling matrix. This would not be news to many historians 'were they not so fetishistically enamoured of the notion of "facts" and so congenitally hostile to "theory" in any form that the presence in a historical work of a formal theory used to explicate the relationship between facts and concepts is enough to earn them the charge of having defected to the despised sociology or having lapsed into the nefarious philosophy of history' (White, op.cit., p.126).

10 Much of this argument is taken from K. Jenkins and P. Brickley, 'On Bias', *History Resource*, 2, 3, 1989.

11 The gist of this section is taken from K. Jenkins and P. Brickley, 'On Empathy', *Teaching History*, 54, April 1989.

12 L. Wittgenstein, *Philosophical Investigations*, Oxford, Blackwell, 1983; O. R. Jones, *The Private Language Argument*, London, Macmillan, 1971.

13 Steiner, *After Babel*, pp.134–6.

14 ibid., p.138.

15 T. Eagleton, *Criticism and Ideology*, London, New Left Books, 1976, p.3.

16 Steiner, *After Babel*, p.18.

17 R. Barthes, in D. Attridge *et al.* (eds), *Post-Structuralism and the Question of History*, Cambridge, Cambridge University Press, 1987, p.3. As we have seen in this section on evidence, Elton's views would run counter both to Barthes' and my own; Elton talks of a 'mass of historical facts' and of the almost unproblematic 'cumulative building up of assured knowledge of both fact and interpretation', G. Elton, *The Practice of History*, London, Fontana, 1969, pp.84–5. See also M. Stanford on historical evidence and construction in *The Nature of Historical Knowledge*, Oxford, Blackwell, 1986, especially chapter 5.

18 See White, op.cit., p.52.

19 T. Eagleton, *Literary Theory*, Oxford, Blackwell, 1983, p.201.

20 See for introductory reading on history and science, P. Gardner, *Theories of History*, London, Collier-Macmillan, 1959.

21 This section draws on White, op.cit., especially chapter 1, 'The Burden of History'.

22 ibid., p.28.

23 H. White, *The Content of the Form*, London, Johns Hopkins University Press, 1987, p.227, note 12.

24 White, *Tropics of Discourse*, pp.46–7.

3   Doing history in the post-modern world

1 A. Callinicos, *Against Post-Modernism*, Oxford, Polity, 1989.

2 J. F. Lyotard, *The Post-Modern Condition*, Manchester, Manchester University Press, 1984.

3 Much of this explanatory story is used to discuss National Curriculum School History in K. Jenkins and P. Brickley, 'Always Historicise . . .', *Teaching History*, 62, January 1991.

4 See G. Steiner, *In Bluebeard's Castle*, London, Faber, 1971, especially chapter 1: 'The Great Ennui'.

5 J. F. Lyotard, 'Time Today', *The Oxford Literary Review*, 11, 1–2, 1989, 3–20, at 12.

6 F. Jameson, 'Post-modernism, or, the Cultural Logic of Late Capitalism', *New Left Review*, 146, 1984. See also P. Dews (ed.), *Habermas: Autonomy and Solidarity*, London, Verso, 1986.

7 Steiner, op. cit., p.66.

8 See Callinicos, op.cit., especially chapter 5: 'So What Else Is New?', pp.121–71.

9 For a general view of post-modernism see D. Harvey, *The Condition of Post-Modernity*, Oxford, Blackwell, 1989.

10 Callinicos, op.cit., p.18.

11 R. Rorty, *Contingency, Irony and Solidarity*, Cambridge, Cambridge University Press, 1989, especially the Introduction.

12 P. Widdowson, 'The Creation of a Past', *The Times Higher Education Supplement*, 3.11.90. See also P. Widdowson (ed.), *Re-reading English*, London, Methuen, 1982.

13 Widdowson, *The Times Higher Education Supplement*.

14 See in particular T. Bennett, *Outside Literature*, London, Routledge, 1990, especially chapter 3 (Literature/History) and chapter 10 (Criticism and Pedagogy: The Role of the Literary Intellectual). Bennett's arguments for a type of post-Marxism and beyond versus post-modernism is interesting and to the point *vis-à-vis* 'the nature of history', wrestling, as he does, with the past as a discursive construct yet wanting it to somehow prevent any sort of discursive practice appropriating it at will. See also, for an attempt to produce a form of solidarity that accepts contingency, irony and freedom and yet which tries to discourage this from becoming 'anything goes', Rorty's really quite brilliant (liberal) work, op.cit.

15 R. Young, *Untying the Text*, London, Routledge and Kegan Paul, 1981, p.viii.

16 For a wide-ranging and thought-provoking discussion and critique of flabby notions of democracy, empowerment, alignment and emancipation, see Bennett, op.cit., chapters 9 and 10. See also the post-Marxist discursive approach of C. Mouffe and E. Laclau in *Hegemony and Socialist Strategy*, London, Verso, 1985, which Bennett analyses in chapter 10, deepening the 'solidarity' problematics of democracy etc. only gestured towards in this book.

17 On this see White's comments that, unlike the twentieth century's prejudice for empirical history as the sole access to reality, the great philosophers of history (Vico, Hegel, Marx, Nietzsche, Croce) and the great classic writers of historiography (Michelet, Carlyle, Ranke, Droyson, Burckhardt) at least 'had a rhetorical self-consciousness that permitted them to recognise that any set of facts was variously,

and equally legitimately, describable, that there is no such thing as a single correct description of anything, on the basis of which an interpretation of that thing can *subsequently* be brought to bear. They recognise, in short, that all original descriptions ... are already interpretations' (H. White, *Tropics of Discourse*, London, Johns Hopkins University Press, 1978, p.127).

18 P. Rieff, *The Triumph of the Therapeutic*, London, Penguin, 1973, *passim*.

Index